STUDIES IN MODERN EUROPEAN LITERATURE
AND THOUGHT

General Editor:
ERICH HELLER
Professor of German
in the University College of Swansea

ANDRÉ GIDE

ANDRÉ GIDE

BY

ENID STARKIE

BOWES & BOWES
CAMBRIDGE

First published in 1953 in the Series
Studies in Modern European Literature and Thought
by Bowes & Bowes Publishers Limited, Cambridge

Printed in the Netherlands
by Joh. Enschedé en Zonen, Haarlem

For
EVANGELINE AND JAMES OLMSTED
A small token of friendship in gratitude
for many things

CONTENTS

André Gide was not only one of the greatest European writers of our time, he was as well one of its main forces. He touched the literature of every country at many points, and not only the literature, but the individual as well, all over the world, even in countries so far distant as Japan. 'There are writers', says François Mauriac, 'the meeting with whom can decide the course of a whole life'. Gide was one of these and I myself can still remember vividly the spiritual shock I received when, at the age of fifteen, I picked up one of his works in a second-hand book-shop on the quays in Dublin. It was the sudden opening of a door, an immediate liberation. It seemed to me that, in a single day, I had been completely transformed. I had never heard of Gide, and only learned of his significance years later when I became a student in Paris. Then I discovered that that very book, *Les Nourritures Terrestres,* had exercised the same influence on most members of my generation in post-war France. In those days Gide's influence was considered pernicious, but since then he has been sanctified by being granted the degree of Doctor of Letters, *Honoris Causa,* by the University of Oxford in 1947—the first honour he had ever received though he was seventy-eight at the time—which was followed in the same year by the Nobel Prize for literature.

It would seem at first sight that it should not be an arduous task to produce a study of Gide, an author who has written nearly a million words of an intimate Journal, as well as several volumes of autobiography, and whose every work was moreover undertaken with the avowed purpose of discovering himself. But, in spite of his frankness and outspokenness, Gide leaves many important episodes so shrouded in a haze of vagueness and uncertainty that it is very difficult to be sure of what has really happened, and diverse interpretations are possible. Indeed he says no less than the truth when he declares 'it is my reticences that are most passionate'. Significant amongst these are those concerning his relationship with his wife, which he calls 'the secret drama of my life'; and he admits that because of his reticence on this important subject his Journal is blinded, with only a hole where the heart should be. This is indeed a tragic admission from a sincere diarist. He calls his attachment for her the secret of all his indecision. In spite of the new light thrown on this subject by the posthumous work, *Nunc manet in te,* the mystery remains as impenetrable as ever.

He has told us much about his homosexuality, but I have never felt personally that this problem is as serious as he thought himself, or would have us believe; not as serious as it need have been if his emotional experience had been different at a critical stage in his development. Later it was as if, deliberately, he sought to be a martyr for this stronghold of prejudice and hypocrisy, the martyr and not the unwilling victim as Oscar Wilde had been. He has told us much about this topic but, on the other hand, he has given no clue to his feelings for the mother of his child, and he has destroyed much of what he wrote about his wife. Normally such questions would not concern the critic, but with a writer like Gide who professes—and indeed practises—frankness in other equally delicate matters, this mixture of reticence and outspokenness is intriguing, and is significant and revealing psychologically.

Although he has written so much about himself, I have never felt that Gide wanted his readers to know him fully; or rather he became afraid and anxious when people began to interpret him—as indeed who does not—and he cries 'Do not understand me so quickly!' In these confessions that he pours out to us he does not provide us with ammunition to use against him, but rather builds up ramparts against us. He wants us to know only the picture that he himself paints. I remember the first time that I went to see him, and he was as charming as I subsequently discovered he was always to everyone. He sat there bending forward with eagerness and sympathetic understanding, anxious that I should feel completely at my ease with him. His smile was of the kindest as he talked freely to me and answered all my questions, but I felt, nevertheless, that I was getting nowhere at all. He seemed to be vanishing further and further behind that smoke-screen of sincere and friendly words and charm, until I felt that I could no longer see him. I tried to resist the overwhelming charm of his personality, to peer into the mist and to seize hold of the elusive figure which seemed to appear and disappear like the Cheshire Cat in *Alice in Wonderland*. In the same way as the smile sometimes appeared without the Cat, I felt that Gide's charming smile was hovering disembodied before me. All my will-power was concentrated in a desperate effort to keep him before me in a concrete form, when suddenly I heard the door behind me open and an old friend of his appeared. This put an end to our conversation. I have often wondered since whether he might not have, like officials in their offices, a hidden bell beneath the ledge of the desk which, on being pressed, rang in another room, whenever he felt that he was slipping out of his own control, and into someone else's nets.

On that first meeting what struck me most about him was the serenity of his expression, and this surprised me, for the picture I had formed of him from his books was of a tormented and anxious being. His works had become for our anguished generation of the post-war years the expression of the new 'Mal du Siècle'. This psychological climate—often called 'angst'—is typical of the Gidian atmosphere and could be called 'Gidism' just as 'Rousseauism' is the influence of Rousseau during the early years of the nineteenth century. This was, however, not the atmosphere radiated by Gide when I met him first twenty years ago, but an earlier one. There was in him the paradox that, at the very moment when he had achieved serenity in

8

himself, his earlier works were beginning to exercise a deep influence over the youth of the country. After the First World War, in the general shipwreck of old values, the world was facing the same problems which had preoccupied him when he began to write as a young man, and then the works which he had written thirty years before became widely known and were the most vital influence on the rising generation; Gide himself by that time, however, had left that phase far behind him and was displeased whenever it was recalled to him.

In spite of its many contradictions there is one striking characteristic which runs through Gide's work in all its many phases, a deep embedded shining seam; his quality as a moralist, passionately interested in the problem of sin, what it is and where it hides itself, especially in the apparently virtuous and complacent. He describes himself as watching people coming out of Church on a Sunday, and he says that their thoughts are freshly washed and ironed by the sermon they have just heard and put away tidily in their minds, as in a cupboard. 'I would like to rummage in the bottom-drawer', he declares, 'I've got the key'. This bottom-drawer is the hidden part of man's nature. As a young man, when he looked at civilisation, he was appalled by the pressure of outworn codes on the individual personality —the Church, society, political theories—, and he considered that, in his attempt to conform, the individual was obliged to develop an outward personality, a counterfeit personality. Discovery of our unacted desires, emancipation from the counterfeit personality, Gide thought, would bring freedom and fulfilment to the individual. It is the inner personality, beneath the counterfeit one, which he always tried to reach; that inner reality where good and evil overlap as in a marriage of Heaven and Hell. In reaching that inner personality he stirs up its troubled depths, drags up from the thick overlaying mud the hidden motives. This is for him the really fertile soil, the one which, in a state of nature, is overrun by exuberant vegetation and which must be cleared before it can be cultivated. He considered that those who had first studied man's nature did so only where it was most easily accessible and that only very gradually did psychologists come to realise all the hidden possibilities in man. All the troubled, tortured and distressed beings are those who interest Gide because he believes that more can be expected from them, when the subterranean forces have been liberated and subdued, than from the complacent. So he studies cases of disconcerting behaviour, cases of apparent wrong-doing; he observes all the idiosyncracies, the nervous tics, as signs which reveal the hidden obsessions; he studies all these unconscious gestures as evidence, just as a detective might look for fingerprints, or analyse grains of dust or tufts of hair. Most of the characters in Gide's writings have some maladjustment, or psychological flaw, which drives them to their doom, and often to the destruction of others as well.

It is impossible, in a short monograph, to give a satisfactory full-length portrait of Gide and of his works. He was in his eighty-second year when he died; his first work appeared in 1891 and following it he published eighty odd volumes. There are many aspects which might be considered. He could be studied as a novelist, a short-story writer, a dramatist or essayist; he could be analysed as an accomplished prose artist or a humourist; as a diarist he has no peer and he is important also as a moralist and psychologist. Any one of these aspects could become the subject of a whole book. To attempt to deal with all at once—as indeed one must if the picture is to have verisimilitude—is to produce only a tangled skein; but then Gide is a very tangled skein, the biographer's despair, the most baffling and fascinating figure in modern literature. 'Is it my fault', he asks, 'if God took great pains to have me born between two stars, fruit of two races, of two provinces and of two creeds?' He means to indicate that his father was a protestant from the South and his mother a Catholic from Normandy; but this suggestion is, however, not quite accurate, for his mother was also a protestant by breeding though from Catholic stock. He was born, as he says, between two stars, on November 22nd, when Scorpio yields the place to Sagittarius.

This little monograph, promised before Gide died and finished in May 1952, the publication of which has been unfortunately delayed through unforeseen circumstances, is intended only as a preliminary sketch for a later full-length portrait. The time is however not ripe for that; we are too near the subject as yet, and the dust from Death's chariot wheels, which still obscures our vision, must first be allowed to settle. It has moreover stirred up all the vicious blowflies which always swarm round the remains of the illustrious dead, and only when they are sated will it be possible to gauge what will survive.

Narcissus Speaks

André Gide was born on November 22nd, 1869. His father, Paul Gide, a professor of Law at the University of Paris, was appointed to the Chair of Roman Law three years after the birth of his only child. He came of protestant stock from Uzès, near Nîmes in Provence, which, since the Reformation, had been a strong centre of Huguenots. His own father, Tancrède Gide, an austere and devout man who devoted his life to good works, did not live to know any of his grandchildren; he died prematurely, refusing to call in a doctor because it was, he declared, contrary to God's intentions. He had been greatly admired and respected by all those who came into contact with him, and his son, Paul, was said to resemble him in many respects—he certainly shared his reputation for honour and integrity and was called 'vir probus' by his colleagues at the École de Droit. One summer, when on holiday in Normandy, he was introduced to a rich heiress called Juliette Rondeaux. She had the reputation of being a spoilt young woman who was very difficult to please since she had refused many eligible suitors and was now no longer young, but she fell passionately in love with the earnest young professor who seemed to share her serious view of life and of its duties and responsibilities. They were married in February 1863 when he was thirty-one and she twenty-eight, but they were to wait six years for the birth of their only child.

Juliette Rondeaux came from a long established bourgeois family in Rouen—there had been Rondeaux of substance as early as the seventeenth century who, by degrees, had accumulated a large fortune through their shrewd business sense and thrifty ways. Edouard Rondeaux, Gide's grandfather, although born a Catholic, was himself a liberal free-thinker who married a protestant and then allowed his children to be brought up as protestants, but one of his sons eventually became converted to Catholicism. He had five children of whom one was Gide's mother and another the father of his cousin Madeleine, his closest friend in childhood and eventually his wife, who remained, to the end of his life, his only great love.

Thus André Gide, on both sides of his family, came from austere, Godfearing protestants whose religious fervour was coloured—or discoloured—by puritanism.

He was born in Paris, in a top-floor flat in the Rue de Médicis, near the corner of the Boulevard Saint Michel, where he could peer, from his window, into the depths of the Luxembourg Gardens and launch paper-darts right over the intervening square, which used to become entangled in the branches of the chestnut trees in the Gardens. He remembered little of his life in that flat, he tells us in his autobiography, little except the reprehensible habits he indulged in with the concierge's little son, hidden under the long, heavy table-cloth of the dining room table; he remembered also the sandcastles made by some children in the Gardens, which he had stamped underfoot one day when he had refused to play with them. These memories remained deeply burnt into his memory as signs of early depravity —though no rational reader would regard them so seriously.

He was six when his parents moved to the Rue de Tournon, to a big flat on the second floor in a house at the corner of the Rue Saint Sulpice. There his chief memory was of his father's large study which he always entered as solemnly and as seriously as if he were going to Church; he remembered the thick pile of the carpet which mysteriously deadened his footfalls, and the calf-bound volumes with their gold lettering and tooling. His father there began to take an interest in his progress and used to read to him, not the insipid children's books current at the time, but Homer, Molière and the *Arabian Nights*. He read him also *The Book of Job* and thus started his son's life-long passion for the Bible. Gide also remembered walks in the summer evenings with his father, when work was over and supper had not been too long delayed. They walked through the Gardens in the dusk, until the roll of the drum gave notice that the gates were closing. He remembered afterwards looking through the railings at the empty park shrouded in mystery.

With so many uncles and aunts on his mother's side there was a great choice of places where he could visit during the holidays. The summer was spent at La Roque, a property inherited by his mother from her father. It was a castle, some parts of which dated back to the sixteenth century, but most of which had been rebuilt in 1803 in the same style. It was surrounded by a moat and he liked to imagine that he was living on an island. He used its setting in two of his novels—in *L'Immoraliste*, and more fully in *Isabelle*. The New Year's holidays he used to spend at Rouen with his Catholic uncle, whose children were much older than he and so no use as playmates, but he played with the daughters of his uncle Émile—Jeanne, Valentine and Madeleine. They were his closest friends and he went often to visit them in their country house at Cuverville, which their father had inherited from his father, and which was to become Gide's home for many years when it belonged to his wife. It is a pleasant well-proportioned eighteenth-century house with romantically laid-out gardens, and Gide used it as a setting for his most perfect work, *La Porte Étroite*. At Easter he used to visit his paternal grandmother in Uzès, and his most vivid memory of that house was connected with a marble which he discovered one day embedded in a knot-hole in a door, and which the maid told him his father had put there as a child and had then been unable to remove it. Gide brooded over this for a whole year before he went there for his next visit; he had allowed one of his finger-nails to grow unusually long and, as soon as he got to his grandmother's house, he inserted it into the hole and levered the marble out. But, as soon as he had succeeded, he was bitterly disappointed for it was only an ordinary black marble, without any mystery or romance, so he slid it back into its cavity and told no one of his exploit. He cut his nail, feeling a bitter sense of disillusionment.

At the age of eight Gide was sent to the École Alsacienne, but his parents were later requested to remove him for a time on account of what were called his evil habits, which he made no attempt to conceal since he did not know that they were wrong.

In 1880, when Gide was eleven, his father died of intestinal tuberculosis and henceforth he was left to his mother's care, whose chief joy and concern he became, her most precious treasure. She had, to help and advise her in this task, her own governess, Anna Shackleton, the daughter of a Scots engineer who had helped to build the Paris-Havre railway. Later Gide bore in his character and personality the stigma of a man brought up exclusively by women. Anna Shackleton encouraged his taste for natural history and botany, which he revealed as early as four years old—; for his mother, once writing to his father, described his habit of standing stock-still deep in contemplation of the behaviour of snails. This interest for botany and zoology lasted him all through his life and many traces are to be found scattered through his *Journal*.

After the death of her husband Madame Gide moved again, to a larger flat in the Rue de Commailles, because one of her sisters told her that she owed it to herself, and to her son, to have a carriage entrance.

Gide's school life was much interrupted during his mother's widowhood. He spent most of one year at Rouen where he shared his cousins' tutor; the following year, perhaps because his mother did not want him to forget his father's family, he lived with his uncle Charles Gide who was a professor at the University of Montpelier, and he was sent to school in the town. Then, for the first time in his life, he became aware of the differences between various religious persuasions and of the bitterness of religious strife, for he was mercilessly bullied by the boys on account of his protestant faith. To avoid returning to school he simulated illness, and it was diagnosed as a nervous ailment; but it is not certain that he was really malingering since various doctors pronounced his complaint authentic and he was henceforth treated with added care so that, even after his return to Paris, he was kept away from school and taught by a succession of inefficient tutors.

When he was thirteen he experienced the great shock which altered his life and gave it a new orientation. He had always played with the daughters of his maternal uncle Émile, but hitherto it had been Jeanne whom he had preferred, since her hobbledehoy ways were more in sympathy with his own. Then

13

one evening, after he had gone home to his uncle Henri with whom he was staying, he did not find him there and returned to his uncle Émile's house, intending to take his cousins by surprise. He found no one about in the house but he crept softly upstairs to the girls' rooms and discovered Madeleine kneeling, weeping by her bedside. He was about to run away but she called to him and then revealed the cause of her grief. She had discovered the infidelity of her mother, she alone of all the family knew it, and she had to keep this secret to herself. It was a grievous burden for an innocent and sensitive child of fifteen to bear, and Gide then suddenly realised why, for so long now, she had seemed unhappy and grave beyond her years. He fell in love with her immediately, although he was only thirteen, and felt that the whole of his life and love should be devoted to curing the intolerable sorrow which dwelt in her. He realised, in a flash, that up to that day he had only been wandering in the outer darkness, but now he discovered the aim and the devotion of his whole life, its mystic orientation. He hid his love for her, but knew that it would never die and that one day he would marry her. He used this scene twice, first in *La Porte Étroite* and then in his autobiography, *Si le Grain ne meurt*.

Shortly after this event one of Gide's older cousins managed to persuade his mother to allow him free access to his father's library and he began to develop his own taste in literature. But, whatever he read, the thought of Madeleine always followed him, and against the passages which he thought would please her in the books he read, he put her initials. He began to correspond with her and to make her the confidante of his deepest thoughts and preoccupations. She encouraged him to read the Bible and his love for her became blended with his love for God. He appears as a grave and innocent youth who read his Bible whenever he could and carried a New Testament everywhere with him. He used to mortify his flesh in order to make himself more worthy of her. He would lie at night, like a Carmelite, on bare boards, and rise in the dark to pray. He used to get up at dawn, bathe in ice-cold water, and read some chapters of the Scriptures before he went to his studies.

Even as a small child Gide had shown aptitude for music, and after his mother had taken him to Rubenstein's recitals in 1883, when he was fourteen, and to the Pasdeloup orchestral concerts the following year, he became passionately interested in music —especially in the piano—and, under the teaching of La Nux, whom he portrayed in the person of La Pérouse in *Les Faux Monnayeurs*, he seemed bent on making music his profession.

When he was eighteen, after intermittent attendance at school, Gide returned to the École Alsacienne for his final year, to work for his Baccalauréat. In his class there was the future poet Pierre Louys. Up to the time of Gide's arrival Louys had always been first in the literature class and he was held by his schoolmates to be a genius. One day, however, the master, to the great surprise of everyone, announced: 'First in the class Gide, and second Louÿs'. All the glances of the boys were fixed on Gide in amazement and he blushed with embarrassment. However, what worried him most was how Louÿs would take his deposition, for he had felt drawn towards him for some time and had been trying to gather the courage to approach him. Now there was this unfortunate episode of the change in the class order, and he felt that he could no longer take the first step.

It was Louÿs himself, however, who made advances by coming up to him and asking him what he was reading. It happened to be a book of poems by Heine and this broke the ice, for Louÿs's ambition was to become a poet. Thereafter they became friends, and he was the first close friend that Gide had ever had, except his cousins. They exchanged poems as they walked together in the woods of Meudon and Chantilly, and Gide confessed to his friend, what he had never yet told anyone, his love for Madeleine and his ambition to write a work which would enshrine that devotion; how he would show it to her, and how then she would love him and consent to marry him.

In July 1889 Gide sat for his Baccalauréat and failed, but he scraped through in October, at the second attempt, and then signed on as a student at the Sorbonne with the presumed purpose of reading for the Licence of philosophy. His studies were, however, the least of his preoccupations. He describes in the first entry of his *Journal* how he climbed to the sixth floor of a house in the Rue Monsieur le Prince, to seek suitable accommodation for a literary Cénacle, and how, looking out of the window into the street, he had thrown down the same challenge to Paris as Rastignac in *Père Goriot* when he had gazed over the city from the cemetery of Père Lachaise.

Gide however found that he could not work in Paris, and he retired to a village near the Forest of Compiègne and later to Lake Annecy; but by the summer of 1890 he was back again in Paris, having almost completed his first work which was finished by the autumn. This was *Les Cahiers d'André Walter*. A recent biographer of Gide, George Painter, has given a new explanation of the name of 'André Walter'. He derives it from the name of a prominent protestant evangelical worker, Henriette André-Walther, who lived from 1807 to 1886 and whose biography was published in 1889, just at the time that Gide was planning his own work.

André Walter is a pious young man, innocent and inexperienced, deeply in love with his orphan cousin Emmanuèle, who is also his adopted sister. Most readers have concluded that this name is that of Gide's own cousin, since in his *Journal* he always refers to her as 'Em'. But this abbreviation is only a pun on the pronunciation of the first initial of her name. André Walter's mother is opposed to a match between her son and her niece and, on her death-bed, she makes him promise to renounce her and bethrothes her to another young man. All three young people kneel and pray at her bedside. Six months after the death of her adopted mother, Emmanuèle marries André Walter's rival and, in order to forget his grief, he begins to write a book. It is written in two note-books—hence the 'cahiers' in the title—one of which is white and the other black. The white one is the colour of renunciation and chastity, and in it André Walter retraces the development of his love for his cousin, many episodes of which recall Gide's own life. He decides then that he will write a novel—many of Gide's works deal with characters who are also writing books which will relate the story of their lives. He hopes that, since he must lose Emmanuèle, he will find God. Just as he is on the point of beginning his novel, news is brought to him that his cousin has died. His sacrifice, he thinks, has been in vain. He begins the black note-book, the colour of mourning and despair. His novel will now be the story of an inner conflict, the conflict between the soul and the body, and it will end with the hero's insanity. It is then a race between André Walter himself and his creation Allain as to which of them will go mad first. Allain wins by a neck, but his creator is not far behind, for he falls ill of brain-fever—that complaint so favoured by inexperienced novelists—and dies on finishing his book.

The *Cahiers d'André Walter* was a book into which Gide poured himself, his reading, his ideals, his struggles and aspirations. It was intended to be a statement of his love for his cousin, a declaration to her, but also a warning of what might happen if she refused him. In this book became focussed and crystallised his view of love for a woman, and it is possible to believe that here begins psychological trouble for him, in his obsession with disembodied and spiritualized love. It was the passionate and adoring love of a young man for a woman somewhat older than himself, whom he idolised but to whom he was rarely able to draw near, through timidity and diffidence. Emmanuèle-Madeleine became the ideal towards which he looked; but she crystallised also for him the idea of the perfect woman, and that was a pity for she, as well as he, was not emotionally stable or normal—she had her own inhibitions and obsessions, for she had been too deeply branded, when a child, by the circumstances of her mother's infidelity, to accept love easily; she remained frightened of it as a force which would wreak such destruction, and for her passionate love was always Racinian. *Les Cahiers d'André Walter* is a young man's romantic and subjective first work, filled with renunciation and tragic death. It is a promising work but is not, naturally, without the faults of youth and inexperience. Its chief interest today is that it tells us much of Gide himself during this formative period of his life, tells it first-hand and not, as in his autobiography, with the mature reflection of a middle-aged man looking back on his youth.

Les Cahiers d'André Walter was published anonymously, at Gide's expense, first in February 1891 in an edition of seventy copies which the author soon afterwards destroyed; but a new edition appeared in April. In one copy of the first edition the heroine's name is given as Madeleine. The book was a complete failure. Nevertheless, although it did not please the public, it opened to its author the doors of Mallarmé's Tuesday evenings in the Rue de Rome, where he was introduced by Pierre Louÿs. Inspired by this Cénacle he produced, in little more than a week, the *Poésies d'André Walter*, which was published, anonymously, as a posthumous work in 1892. Gide was later to claim that these poems were too good for a silly fool like André Walter, but to most of his admirers the *Cahiers* is a vastly more interesting and fruitful work, for he was not a natural poet.

Les Cahiers d'André Walter did not however have on Madeleine the effect Gide had hoped, for it seems to have frightened her. He proposed marriage to her but she refused him on the plea that she did not yet feel prepared to marry anyone. Had she accepted him his later life—and hers too—might well have been vastly different.

At the end of 1890, while *Les Cahiers d'André Walter* was printing, Gide went to Montpelier to see Paul Valéry to whom he had a letter of introduction from Pierre Louÿs. Gide's conversation with the poet inspired his next work, *Le Traité du Narcisse*, which he published under his own name. In the public gardens of Montpelier there stands a monument dedicated to the memory of the daughter of the poet Young, inscribed 'Placandis Narcissae Manibus'—'For the peace of the shade of Narcissa'. The name 'Narcissa' recalled to the two young men the name of Narcissus and they each wrote a work inspired by him —Valéry his poem *Narcisse parle*, and Gide his treatise on Symbolism, *Traité du Narcisse*. The latter relates how Narcissus, in a desire to know himself, contemplates his own reflection in the river of Time, and dreams of lost perfection. The river flows back to the past, to the Garden of Eden where Adam, reigning alone in a state of perfect bliss, in a moment of idleness breaks a twig from the tree Ygdrasil. Immediately time is born and imperfection. The tree is blasted and Adam is split in two, and left forever longing to rejoin his other half. Henceforth man has a nostalgic yearning for perfection which is unattainable. Narcissus, trying in vain to embrace his image in the stream, decides that truth and perfection cannot be possessed but only perceived, by intuition, through their symbols. The treatise contains an excellent definition of the doctrine of the Symbolist Movement in France. Gide's treatise was published in January 1891 in a review, and so it is in fact his first published work, though bibliographers do not seem to have noticed this fact.

Gide had thought that by writing *Les Cahiers d'André Walter* he would purge himself of anxiety and distress, but he found that he could not escape. He threw himself into frivolity and pleasure because Madeleine would have nothing to do with him or his book; yet none of this satisfied him and, at the end of the year, he returned to God for help, thinking that he had strayed too far. The thought of his cousin still followed him and he wrote in his *Journal:* 'I thank thee Lord, that the only feminine influence on my delighted soul, which wished for no other, is the influence of Em. I take joy in thinking that if she were to return to me I should have no secrets from her.' She had broken off her correspondence with him after she had refused him.

In November 1892 Gide was called up for his military service, but he was soon invalided out of the army on the score of a predisposition to tuberculosis.

His next work, a novel called *Voyage d'Urien*, was published in 1893, but its final chapter was printed separately in December 1892 under the title *Voyage à Spitzbergen*. When he showed this in manuscript to Mallarmé he noticed an expression of perplexity on the face of the Master, and later learned the reason. 'You gave me a fright', said the poet, as he returned him his script, 'I really thought you had been there'. He imagined that he had been given a travel-book to read but he, the poet of absence and non-fulfilment, was delighted with a journey its author had never taken. *Le Voyage d'Urien* is the first of Gide's works in which irony and satire are found, which will be marked characteristics of some of his later works. In this new mood we may perhaps discern the influence of Oscar Wilde, whom he first met in 1891 and then saw fairly continuously for some time. This was at the height of Wilde's fame and prosperity, many years before his downfall. His influence was to wean Gide from pre-occupation with purely ethical values.

In 1893 Gide composed *La Tentative Amoureuse* in which he deliberately dissociated love, which is a spiritual affection, from desire, which is a physical pleasure. The hero longed for love but was afraid of physical possession; the heroine, however, insisted on giving herself to him and all the summer they experienced the increasing boredom which comes from love's pleasures too lightly snatched, and finally, in the autumn, they parted.

All through 1893 Gide was restless and chafing against restrictions; he was longing to escape, to find new Gods, and to enjoy life without always wondering whether what he was doing was right or wrong. He wanted particularly to experience the joys of the flesh and to escape from the puritan chastity of his up-bringing. 'I lived until the age of twenty-three completely virgin', he wrote, 'and utterly depraved; crazed to such a point that eventually I came to seek everywhere some piece of flesh on which to press my lips'.

In October 1893 emancipation came when Paul-Albert Laurens, the son of the painter, invited him to accompany him to North Africa. Gide set off, as he says in his autobiography, as if in search of the Golden Fleece, which was sexual experience, and he hoped thereafter to find classical balance and harmony. He felt that this journey was an important step forward in his life, and to mark its significance, he left his Bible, from which he had not been parted for a single day for many years, at home. It had been his source of strength, his daily bread, but precisely because he had relied on it so much, he intended now to wean himself from it. It was however not without a painful wrench.

II

The Fruits of the Earth

Gide spent the summer holidays of 1893 at Yport with the family of Paul-Albert Laurens who had been his schoolmate at the École Alsacienne and had now won a travelling scholarship in painting. He chose to visit Algeria and invited Gide to accompany him. This was the first of Gide's many visits to North Africa.

The trip unfortunately started badly. At Toulon, where they spent the night, Gide, who had caught a chill, was beginning to feel very ill. He did not mention this to his friend, but thought for a moment that it might be wise to abandon the trip altogether; yet he went on, meaning to turn back if he got any worse. They had a fine crossing and as they entered Tunis harbour Gide had the impression of coming into the land of the Arabian Nights, of which he had dreamed in his childhood. The golden flying fish and array of camels on the quayside all seemed to him romantic and mysterious. They first turned towards the south, through the desert, but the weather was bad, and when they reached Susa Gide seemed very ill. Laurens called in a doctor who took a serious view of his state of health and dissuaded them from going any further through the desert. They spent six days at Susa and there occurred an episode which was to be significant for Gide's future development. Laurens used to go out painting every day and Gide, when he felt well enough, accompanied him. One day, after he had allowed his friend to outdistance him, he tells us—or rather hints—that he discovered his true nature, his homosexual leanings. It was the little Arab boy, who accompanied him to carry his rug, and guessing more about him than he knew himself, who initiated him. When he met Laurens again he did not tell him of his experience, but buried it in his heart, not willing to face it yet.

Since the two young men could not continue their journey through the desert, they decided to spend the winter at Biskra, and while Laurens used to sally forth with easel and paints, to make pictures, Gide would sit in the warmth of the hotel terrace and try to regain his health.

Then Laurens decided that it was time that they carried out the plan which had been one of their main reasons for going to Africa, for he was as anxious as his friend to find sexual experience. Gide was now however less interested than formerly, but thought that with normal experience he might forget his unnatural cravings. Laurens, who had met an Arab girl and fallen in love with her, now suggested that they should share her, and that she should come to their lodgings since Gide was not yet strong enough to go to hers. The experience was not however successful as far as Gide was concerned, for in her arms he thought only of the Arab boy at Susa.

Gide's health did not improve very quickly and when one day he had a haemorrhage, Laurens became so alarmed that he mentioned it in a letter to his parents who thought it only right to inform Gide's mother. She came post-haste to Biskra to nurse him, bringing with her the old family servant Marie. One morning, when she had awakened early and was seated at her window, she saw the Arab girl creeping out of Laurens' room at dawn; she questioned her son about this and he, not wishing his friend alone to bear the blame, confessed to her that he too had shared Merriem. His mother wept, he wept with her, and the result was that they ceased asking the girl to their house, but went to hers instead.

By the spring Gide was better and he felt an upsurging love of life, a longing to enjoy it to the full. It was then that he composed his *Ronde de la Grenade* which he later incorporated in *Les Nourritures Terrestres*.

Seeing him now so much better his mother returned to France, and Gide and Laurens left Africa to travel in Sicily and Italy, visiting Rome and other cities, and finally reaching Florence where they encountered Oscar Wilde. After that they separated, and Gide went to Geneva to consult a doctor recommended by his uncle, who informed him that there was nothing wrong with his lungs but that his nerves were overstrung. Gide then returned to Paris feeling like a man reprieved, for he had been much afraid of having contracted tuberculosis. In Paris, however, he felt as Lazarus must have felt when he came back from the dead, that no one understood him. He returned to the stifling atmosphere of the Paris salons where, as he says, 'the agitation of each one stirred up the stench of death'. He went on to say that it would have brought him to the brink of suicide had it not been for the escape he found in describing it ironically in his next work, *Paludes*. This is the story of a young man who is writing a book, also called *Paludes*. It tells of the life of the animals who live in dark caves and lose their sight through not using it. It is one of Gide's most brilliantly written works and, when he had finished it, he felt that he had liberated himself from all that had previously made him suffer. He believed that he could now safely return to North Africa.

He felt Blidah bitterly cold with the icy wind blowing, and moreover could find no satisfactory lodgings; he was just on the point of leaving the hotel when he saw written on a slate in the office the names of Oscar Wilde and Lord Alfred Douglas. When he had met Wilde previously he had known nothing of his reputation, except as a man of letters, but since then rumours of his habits had reached him; and now, fearful for his own reputation, he erased his name from the slate, paid his bill, and went off to the station. Then, with characteristic Gidian scruples, he became ashamed of his cowardice and returned to the hotel. When he met Wilde later in the evening with Lord Alfred he found him much changed, more vulgar and blatant in flaunting his homosexual habits, for it was as if the presence of his friend urged him on to greater daring. Lord Alfred took it for granted that Gide was of the same persuasion for he said to him: 'These guides are stupid, they will insist on taking one to cafés full of women. I hope that you are like me, I have a horror of women and like only boys!' Wilde also, to his surprise for he had never mentioned the subject to him, assumed the same attitude and one evening, after his friend had left, took him to a certain café and procured a boy for him. Gide wrote subsequently that he had found with the youth a joy and serenity which he had never yet experienced. This time he had no pangs of conscience and was at peace with himself, now that he had openly admitted his leanings. In this state of bliss he conceived *Les Nourritures Terrestres* and wrote several passages of it; although it was not finished then it belongs to this moment of happiness and freedom. The work springs primarily from his discovery of the liberation which came through sexual experience. It is an answer to the problem of *Paludes*.

In writing *Les Nourritures Terrestres* Gide intended to preach evasion from the shackles of convention and usage. 'One must act', he says, 'without pausing to consider whether the action is good or evil; love without troubling whether it is good or evil'. And again: 'Commandments of God, you have made my soul ill, you have surrounded with walls the only springs to quench my thirst'.

Those who disapproved of the work — and there were many— saw in it the glorification of sensuality, the destruction of discipline and authority. These strictures were to annoy Gide, for he knew that his intentions had been pure; and indeed, the pleasures that he advocates are innocent, and not devoid of idealism. The spiritual joys are for him the supreme joys, but he longs for them to be less puritanical and less connected with mortification of the flesh.

In *Les Nourritures Terrestres* Gide addresses the young through Nathanael, who is the symbol of youth; that is why he exercised so great an influence in the nineteen-twenties. He draws them aside when they are weary from reading many books, and from finding nothing in them on which their souls may feed. He tells them that he writes for them alone. Then, having spoken to them, in the hours of sadness and loneliness, he advises them, after finishing his book, to cast it away, to emancipate themselves from it. 'Do not think that your truth can be found by anyone save you. Throw away my book and say to yourself that here is only one of the possible gestures in front of life. Find your own. What someone else could have done as well as you, do not do. Cultivate in yourself only what you feel is nowhere else, and create the most irreplaceable of beings.'

Each youth in the nineteen-twenties, reading these lines, felt that they had been written for him alone, and many were turned into rebels. It is a work calculated to appeal to the young, with its lyrical expression of joy. Those, however, who have reached maturity and who have read Gide's later writings in a classical style of austere beauty, will sometimes find the ecstatic lyricism of *Les Nourritures Terrestres* somewhat too lush, too reminiscent of Walter Pater, and, in spite of its obvious sincerity, it will strike them as somewhat too studied and artificial.

In the midst of composing *Les Nourritures Terrestres* in Biskra Gide was interrupted in March 1895 by his mother, whose letters recalled him because she had been anxious lest he should be becoming too independent, and feared also that he might be enjoying an illicit relationship like the one she had uncovered the previous year. He returned to France and spent some happy weeks with her, amongst the happiest of his life; their only topic of disagreement was the title of his book, which she thought suggested licence. He was serene and contented and looking forward to spending the summer with her at La Roque, where he hoped that Madeleine might join them and that she might now consent to marry him. He was staying with friends while his mother went ahead with Marie to open up the house, when a telegram reached him from the maid telling him that the old lady had had a stroke. He hurried to her but found her dying, and he was not even certain that she still recognised him. She died some days later, in May 1895, not in July as he states in his autobiography.

Gide's grief shattered his recent joy, and he turned to religion once more for comfort, living in an exalted state when all he prayed for was the possibility of sacrificing himself. Then he abandoned the unfinished *Nourritures Terrestres* since it no longer reflected his mood, and conceived his play *Saul* which takes the diametrically opposite view.

Gide was always irritated later when critics praised *Les Nourritures Terrestres* at the expense of his other works, and he himself deplored its influence in the twenties, for by that time he had written many books with other views. In a Preface to an edition in 1927 he declared that it had been the work of a convalescent, and that through it he had regained his health, but that nevertheless it was not his only book and that he refused to be judged by it alone. He declared that the dangers of the doctrine had been so apparent to him that immediately, as an antidote, he had conceived his play *Saul*, the subject of which is precisely the ruin of the soul and the extinction of the personality, the inevitable results of non-resistance to temptation.

All Gide's thoughts at this time were centred on his cousin Madeleine, and he clung to her as to his only hope and ideal. She seemed to him everything that he most admired and needed; she believed in him and in his higher possibilities, whereas he was always uncertain of himself and obsessed by a feeling of guilt. He proposed marriage to her and this time she accepted him.

Gide was subsequently severely criticised for having married her, since by then he was aware of his homosexual leanings; but he did not take the step lightly, and consulted a doctor who assured him that since he loved her, all would be well, and told him that his aberrations were like those of a starving man who had tried to feed on nothing but pickles.

It was not solely on his own account that Gide had wished to marry Madeleine. He hoped that he could now devote his whole life to her and make up to her for the suffering of her girlhood; he longed to give her happiness and to share with her the bliss that he had enjoyed himself for so short a time. But you cannot give happiness, your own form of happiness, to another; it can only grow through fusion, and that did not happen. Their life together did not turn out as Gide had hoped and there was, as will be related later, strife and struggle between them. But she remained the great love of his life, his only really deep emotion. Had he never married her, had he remained single, his work would certainly have been different. It would probably have been the poorer, for it might have lacked its spiritual polarisation.

Gide and Madeleine were married in October 1895 by the same protestant clergyman who had married his parents thirty-two years before. He was twenty-six and she twenty-eight. They set out for a long honeymoon lasting almost six months. They spent the autumn in Switzerland, the early winter in Italy when they visited Florence, Rome and Naples; then they moved south to North Africa which, in spite of his other travels, still beckoned to Gide.

They returned to La Roque in May 1896 and Gide was immediately elected mayor of the commune by an overwhelming majority—the youngest mayor of France. He said later that those who claimed that he was indifferent to the public weal did not realise how much civic zeal he had brought to his arduous duties. He took them very seriously. He joined couples in holy matrimony, frightened hardened alcoholics into reforming, and had cases retried when he thought that there had been a miscarriage of justice.

He spent some of the year also at Cuverville, and there he finished *Les Nourritures Terrestres*, which appeared in April 1897. It fell completely flat, and in ten years only five hundred copies were sold. George Painter relates a joke which he says was current in the offices of his publisher; they used to beg visitors to take away a few of the 'Fruits', saying that they were a glut on the market and would not keep much longer. Gide, however, had his revenge twenty-five years later, when the book became his most popular and influential work.

In the mean time he was also working on *Saul* and on *Le Prométhée mal enchaîné*. They were both finished in 1898; the second was published in 1899, although the first did not appear until 1903.

III

Prometheus Misbound

After his return from his honeymoon Gide was occupied in finishing *Les Nourritures Terrestres*, but he did not seem able to recapture the mood of total joy he had experienced in North Africa. He sought diversion and change in composing *El Hadj*, the treatise of the false prophet, on which he worked in 1896. It relates how a Prince leads his people, with the promise of spiritual joys, to the salt marshes of the Eternal City. On their journey thither he does not permit them to enjoy even the pleasures of the oases in which they rest by night, for fear that they might be turned away from their high purpose. As they reach the borders of the promised land the leader dies and his people are left without a guide. They are led back again to their earthly city by El Hadj who would have them enjoy the pleasures of this world. They are glad of his leadership and are convinced that he is a prophet, but he knows that he is only a false one. Gide here doubts the spiritual as well as the material solution for the problems of life, since both prove disappointing. *El Hadj* was published in 1899, in the same year as *Le Prométhée mal enchaîné*.

Having completed these works Gide took up *Saul* again and finished it in a mood of deep pessimism in 1898. When he had begun *Les Nourritures Terrestres* he had wandered through pleasant paths and by-ways, but he thought now that they had led him only to destruction. He now wanted to prove that those who do not resist temptations will end by being destroyed by them, as well as those who set themselves up as sole judges of their own deeds. All the desires to which, at the time of *Les Nourritures Terrestres*, it had seemed wholesome to yield now came to destroy Saul, and amongst them the one to which Gide had surrendered with such a sense of liberation. Saul was tempted by his dawning passion for David, and he slew his wife because she had discovered his guilty secret. David, however, had also guessed it and then turned against him whom he had previously considered as his Master, and joined forces with his enemies.

After finishing *Saul* Gide grew weary of dwelling on the inevitable retribution which follows sin. There was, as was usual with him, the swing of the pendulum to the other extreme. It was as if he felt that he had been too severe on Saul, who had really been the victim of a cruel and unjust God. He then composed *Le Prométhée mal enchaîné* as an antidote, and it is inspired by the same vein of irony as *Voyage d'Urien* and *Paludes*. Here occurs the first of the 'actes gratuits' of which so much has been written. An 'acte gratuit' is an apparently motiveless action, the freest of all actions, Gide says, the one which separates the man from the beast, for it is performed for no personal—hence limiting—motive. It is the act which man performs with the whole of his personality, with all his characteristics. The most famous one is that in *Les Caves du Vatican* where the hero, without any motive, murders a perfect stranger in a train by hurling him out of the carriage door. Although such an action might, at first sight, appear to be gratuitous, it seems so only because the motive is deeply hidden even from the perpetrator of the deed. Gide was to reach this conclusion later, when he was a member of a jury and had to make decisions on questions of behaviour. He writes of one of these in *L'Affaire Redureau*, the case of a young man who had killed, without apparent motive, seven people. Gide then believed that if the personality had been fully aware of itself, fully co-ordinated, then the crimes would never have been committed; if the personality had been free from the obsessions and inhibitions which had caused psychological maladjustment, then violence might well have never occurred.

The Greek Prometheus has been chained to a mountain by Zeus as a punishment for having tried to increase the freedom of man, and an eagle is sent daily to feed on his liver. Gide's Prometheus, finding his chains, which symbolise his scruples and conventions, irksome, casts them off and descends into the city of modern life, but he does not know where to go. He sits in a café to find out. People pass and the waiter tells him that they are men in search of their personalities. He has with him his eagle which gives him a certain distinction. He has affection for it and feeds it on his flesh so that it grows sleek and beautiful. He does not love man any more, but only the eagle that devours him, that is the special passion that torments him. The eagle also symbolises man's conscience and he must make his peace with it and finally conquer it. Prometheus ends by killing his eagle and eating it. It is with one of its feathers that the author has written his tale.

In spite of its satire and the gaiety of its style, *Le Prométhée mal enchaîné* is serious in intention. It is a further restatement of the thesis of *Les Nourritures Terrestres*, the quest for individual values which were discarded in *Saul*. Here Gide symbolises God as a corpulent and unreasonable banker who performs stupid 'actes gratuits' to the discomforture of man, handing out meaningless retribution and unfair torture. Prometheus, standing for man, is wiser and stronger than he.

With *Le Prométhée mal enchaîné* we come to the end of Gide's discussion of man's solitary destiny, the conquest of personal liberty. Hereafter, for the next twenty years, the problem that will occupy him is the one dealing with his relationship with his wife. He examines then the dangers which beset and threaten the liberty gained. During all these years, in spite of his great love for her and hers for him, he lived in a state of conflict and distress. The problem is not an easy one to clarify for much of it is shrouded in mystery, but everything we read leaves behind it an impression of tragedy and misunderstanding which rouses compassion for these two unhappy beings who loved one another deeply and yet were driven to bring each other much unhappiness and distress. The works that Gide composed from now until the end of the First World War all reflect, from differing angles, the same problem. He worked it out in every aspect, giving it different possibilities and solutions. How was he to reconcile his need for complete individual freedom with his duty to his wife—nay, his deep love for her and anxiety to please her? How reconcile her austerity, even puritanism, with his longing for every kind of experience? The Prodigal son in his tale does return home, but very reluctantly and with the impression of having failed in his purpose by yielding so soon, but he encourages his young brother to escape and warns him not to follow his example.

Every facet of Gide's relationship with his wife is to be found somewhere in his work during these twenty years. He wrote of nothing else. But, since he was a great artist, the scenes and episodes are transfigured and transposed, and the characters become real beings in their own right. They are not wholly himself nor his wife, for he said that what was lacking in each of the characters that he carved from his own flesh was that modicum of common-sense which prevented him from carrying their follies as far as they did. He worked out the problem of his married life as a theorem in each book that he wrote. He studied it from different angles and drew out all the different aspects of that long and painful struggle, particularly in *L'Immoraliste*, *La Porte Étroite* and *La Symphonie Pastorale*. The different contrasting aspects are seen particularly in the first of these works. *L'Immoraliste* is the story of a man who destroys his own and his wife's happiness through his egoistical conception of personal liberty. *La Porte Étroite* tells of a girl who destroys her own happiness and that of the man she loves but never marries, through a false conception of virtue.

There was between him and his wife incessant struggle which was never really resolved. In that conflict what he most feared was to become an unconscious hypocrite. It was to crystallise that terror that he conceived *La Symphonie Pastorale*. Here the 'pasteur', though a good man and frequently actuated by genuine Christian ideals, brings about disaster through his self-deception. Hypocrisy, unconscious or otherwise, was a problem that fascinated Gide and it is the human failing which he attacked most fiercely.

26

The forty-three years of Gide's married life were years of lack of understanding and intimacy. Roger Martin du Gard describes his first visit to Cuverville, and the distant politeness of the pair to one another, the courtesy of casual acquaintances. Neither could draw near the other, and Gide complains several times that nothing was ever brought out in the full daylight, and that there never was between them a frank discussion on anything. Yet every line he ever wrote reflects his longing for sympathy and understanding. He said that every work until *Les Faux Monnayeurs* was written as an appeal to her, but she would never read any for she knew beforehand that she would disapprove. Although she never reproached him openly, her life with him was a long silent reproach for his being as he was, and she did not give him the warmth of understanding which would soften disapproval and make it light to bear. All through his married life he did not cease from longing for that intimacy; it was an open wound which nothing would heal.

In spite of her goodness there was some hard streak in her, as when she deliberately wounded him by giving away a carefully chosen gift. It was as if she would not allow herself to enjoy anything he had given her, nor let him guess her pleasure. She also made it patently clear to him that she did not read his writings by leaving the pages of his contributions uncut in periodicals in which she had read the other articles.

It is not certain whether she ever realised his homosexual tendencies. In his letters to Claudel in 1912 he declares that she is ignorant of the fact and that, as he loves her more than his life, he is always afraid she may learn of it. Yet, when he writes of his honeymoon it would seem impossible that she should still have been in ignorance, as he describes how he neglected her for young artists' models in Italy and how, through the carriage window on the train, he tried to attract the attention of some youths next door. These passages, written after her death in a moment of self-flagellation, do not however ring true.

One has the impression that she lived beside him for more than forty years in silent disapproval which she never openly expressed, loving him deeply, yet always wishing him to be different. There was no doubt that she loved him to the end, although her love was mingled with grief. She said to him once, very much later: 'I owe my greatest joy to you, but also my greatest sadness—the best and the most bitter'.

On several occasions in letters and Journal, Gide declared that he felt no physical desire for her, or for any other woman; but he did not say this at the time of his marriage, only very much later. At first he certainly imagined that women do not feel sexual desire as men do. In his dreams his wife appeared to him as a will o' the wisp always eluding his grasp, and the dream became a nightmare. It is possible to believe that had she been able to break down his reserves they might have reached full happiness. She was the older and he had, all through his child-

27

hood and youth, deferred to her and waited on her command, so that later he found it impossible to take the virile lead which marriage requires, and then took refuge in the excuse of his homosexuality. He suggests, though he does not say so specifically, that the marriage was never consummated, and he takes the full blame for this, attributing it to a definite resolve on his part. He may have preferred this reputation to the one of incapacity—Jerome in *La Porte Étroite*, who is a reflection of Gide himself, gives the impression of impotence. His wife was no help to him. She had her own obsessions and inhibitions. She had a fear of physical passion, wounded as she had been as a girl by her discovery of the change wrought in her own mother through passionate love; and so Gide, afraid of hurting or disgusting her, did not persevere. He tells us that she would have liked a child but was too reserved to let him know this, and so, in unconscious vengeance against him for not having sufficiently loved her—as it must have seemed to her, doubting her charm for him—she did everything she could to destroy the image he once had of her and the things he had loved. She allowed her physical beauty to vanish and no longer cultivated her mind. All he could do was look on in impotent despair. She destroyed her gifts as Alissa did in *La Porte Étroite*. Whenever her shadow passes through the *Journal* we are conscious of anxiety and distress.

Yet she remained for Gide his idol and his ideal of woman, and probably inspired him more than if she had given him peace and contentment. Thinking of her he strove always to be better than he was by nature. These two beings lived side by side for almost half a century, loving one another deeply yet each laying waste the heart of the other.

With this problem we reach a new Gide, preoccupied with psychological more than with lyrical and personal problems. Now, with the opening of the twentieth century, we have, until *Les Faux Monnayeurs* in 1925, his greatest and richest period as a creative artist.

IV

Strait is the Gate

With the new century we reach a fresh phase in Gide's work, a nobler phase than hitherto, where he shows greater mastery as a writer, and greater psychological awareness. He is no longer the artist struggling alone against fate, but a man concerned with the problem of living together with another individual, with whom he must find harmony. There is a corresponding sobering of his lyric style and a pruning away of all previous lusciousness. Now, for the first time, we find André Gide the creator of faultless prose.

Here begins also his period of psychological distress and

'angst', when he floundered in doubts and scruples, and was pulled hither and thither, never knowing whether what he was doing was right or wrong; when the opinions of others had power to wound him deeply.

It is the time also when—as we learn from the *Journal*—to escape from the restrictions, imagined or real, of the conjugal home, he used to wander solitary through the streets of Paris at night, toying, it seems mostly in imagination, with the temptation of furtive homosexual experience. These encounters, if indeed they ever became real, never developed into relationships.

It is at this time that he began to be widely known—and also ostracised.

This period of twenty-five years could be subdivided into two fairly even parts, separated by *Les Caves du Vatican* of 1914.

In the first part Gide was preoccupied with the problem of his marriage and his study of it in his writings. It contains *L'Immoraliste*, *L'Enfant Prodigue*, *La Porte Étroite*, *Isabelle* and the initial conception of *La Symphonie Pastorale* which, by inspiration, belongs to it. Gide declared later that each of his books was a work of criticism. *L'Immoraliste* criticizes a form of individualism; *La Porte Étroite* a mystical and religious tendency; *Isabelle* a kind of romanticism; while *La Symphonie Pastorale* is an indictment of self-deception. He studies the problem of his marriage in all its aspects and purges himself of much perplexity in the process of writing.

L'Immoraliste is the first of these works. Unfortunately, there are no entries in his *Journal* for the time of composition, and we do not know whether they were ever written or whether they were destroyed, and so we have no clue to his state of mind. But, from subsequent entries, and from the testimony of letters, we gather that he became, after his honeymoon, increasingly troubled, and that he suffered a great deal nervously.

L'Immoraliste is written, as are nearly all Gide's works, in the first person. This enabled him to give greater verisimilitude to his writing. The story is not, however, wholly his and many of the episodes which actually did happen in his life have their chronology and emphasis altered. He created his characters from his own flesh and blood, but they are never wholly himself, though, as he admits, he would become them so entirely as he wrote that they seemed to be himself. Then he allowed himself to be carried away to where he would not have gone on his own. He said later that people always insisted on seeing personal declarations of faith and beliefs in the utterances of each of his characters however diverse and contradictory they might be.

In *Les Nourritures Terrestres* Gide had sung lyrically of the necessity for self-realisation and the joys that came therefrom; but in *L'Immoraliste*, on the contrary, he shows these no longer in imagination but in real life, as a problem to wrestle with and solve, and to fit into the frame-work of human relations. His aim now was to study psychologically the effect of these beliefs on human beings. Is it possible, he asks by implication, especially in married life, to live according to the philosophy of *Les Nourritures Terrestres*? The answer to this question is *L'Immoraliste*.

In this tale Gide retraces the stresses and strains of his life with Madeleine. The hero Michel has the same paralysis of the will before his wife. He tries to escape from his bonds but can only do so by hurting, indeed eventually killing, Marceleine. It is emotionally necessary for Gide that she should die, as she symbolises all the restraints against which he had been chafing. But, after she is dead, he is left with guilt and despair.

L'Immoraliste is the first of Gide's works written in limpid and pure prose which does not fall far short of his greatest works; and it is far in advance of any of his previous compositions.

Gide's next works, two short ones, are in the nature of an interlude in his personal problems. They were written as a tribute to Oscar Wilde who had died in 1900 and whose funeral he had been unable to attend on account of absence abroad. They are *In Memoriam* and *De Profundis*, slight essays which study Wilde's personality rather than his writings; but there exists no truer picture of the conversationalist, and that was how Gide chiefly saw him at this time, though later he regretted not having treated his writings more seriously. It was Gide who asked Wilde why his books were not better considering his gifts, and was then answered that he had put his genius into his life and only his talent into his works.

Gide would have liked to write immediately the companion book to *L'Immoraliste*, the reverse of the same medal, *La Porte Étroite*, but he was inhibited for many years. It has usually been argued that the lack of success of the earlier book had discouraged him, but it is more likely that his inhibition was due to that paralysis which always overcame him when he wanted to portray his wife. In *La Porte Étroite* he was obliged to deal with matters which deeply touched his emotions, and the problem was now to show how in the failure of the couple the woman, as well as the man, shared in the blame. He would also, in the portrait of Alissa, have liked to please his wife—or at least not to hurt her. Few of us, however, are satisfied with our portraits by others—even when they are flattering—for they do not correspond to that secret picture we hide in the depths of our heart; we feel that we have not been understood, and to be understood is what, in our blindness, we imagine that we most want. There were scenes which meant much to him and which he could not achieve to his satisfaction, particularly the one where Jerome comes on Alissa weeping over her mother's infidelity, kneeling by her bedside. He wrote the scene again and again without success. In desperation he went to North Africa to seek inspiration, ostensibly to write a travel book, but secretly with the hope of recapturing the joy of *Les Nourritures Terrestres*. It was, however, a book of sadness rather than of joy that he brought back: *Amyntas*, a renunciation of travel.

After this he was drawn back to Cuverville which was now his home until his wife's death, since, after finishing *L'Immoraliste*, he had sold his own property. He set to work on *La Porte Étroite*, and after several years he wrote that he was beginning it again for the fourth time, and he considered giving it up altogether. So difficult did he find it to finish that he interrupted it for a time in 1907 to write, in a few weeks, *Le Retour de l'Enfant Prodigue*. Here the prodigal, after his return, doubts his wisdom and urges his young brother to leave and never to come back. Gide was indeed a prodigal who often, despite his deep love for his wife, felt the pressing need to break away from home. He describes himself as creeping out of Cuverville at dawn, after a sleepless night due to his sorrow at the thought of paining Madeleine, but, at the same time, full of joy at the anticipation of freedom. 'Even at the moment when you were leaving her, you could not hide your joy from her. Why then were you almost irritated that she could not hide her tears from you?'

Gide finally finished *La Porte Étroite* in October 1908. When he had completed it he said that it was like a piece of nougat in which the almonds were good—that is the letters and Alissa's diary—but that the mass which held them together was of poor quality. That is not the opinion generally held, for it is considered to be one of his most perfect works, in style and content.

La Porte Étroite had been conceived many years before, at the same time as *L'Immoraliste*, and he always claimed that they should be taken together. He called them twins and said that they were two facets of the same problem and that, had he been able physically to write them at the same moment, he would have done so. *L'Immoraliste* had shown how one form of egoism, if allowed full licence, would destroy everything. Now he wanted to demonstrate that it is not the egoist alone who is guilty, but that some of the blame must also go to the allegedly virtuous party. In a letter to Claudel he declared that his intention had been to show the error of that heady form of superior infatuation and of contempt for all pleasures of this world. This could, naturally, be mingled with true nobility and greatness.

La Porte Étroite is the most movingly personal of all Gide's work. It mirrors the mystic orientation of his life and his dedication to his cousin. It reflects also his consciousness of failure with her. In real life he may have married her, but he remained, nevertheless, as shut out as the hero of the tale, by the strait gate. Alissa's reluctance to accept Jerome is complex. It was not only that she wished to make a sacrifice of her love to God: there were other obstacles as well. Through the shock she had received as a girl, when she had discovered her mother's infidelity, she had kept a neurotic fear of love as a force that brought destruction. There was also puzzled amazement at, perhaps even contempt of, a love that seemed rooted in impotence. Her religion was her escape and also her excuse, but to see her altering little by little, to see her sacrifice all her gifts of beauty, taste, and intellect in a mistaken idea of virtue, Jerome suffered as Gide declared that he had suffered at a similar diminution in his wife.

Finally, in a scene of great literary and psychological beauty, Alissa says farewell to Jerome, at a little gate leading into the garden, symbolical surely of the strait gate through which he can no longer accompany her. She enters it alone and bids him not try to follow her.

There is a similar little gate at Cuverville, and Gide could never look at it without emotion, for he had lived so intensely these moments with Alissa and Jerome that tears would run down his face as he showed it to visitors. 'I walk here like a ghost', he said, 'in a past that is dead'.

La Porte Étroite is Gide's most exquisitely planned and written work. It has a harmony of style and a unity of action which are truly classical. The psychology too is more sure and subtle than in any of his former novels, and it is not only the two main characters who are drawn with such skill but also the host of different minor ones who make up the complex family circle; all are portrayed with sympathetic understanding and placed in their own correct setting. The tale has only one fault of construction. It would have been truer and more artistic to have ended it with Jerome reading the last entry of Alissa's diary, that she left him in her will, instead of adding the more conventional Epilogue, where he visits her sister ten years afterwards and sees in her room the furniture he had known so well in Alissa's. They talk of bygone days and he realises that he will never forget the past.

To the surprise of everyone the novel sold, and it was the first of Gide's works to reach a wide public. His publishers, thinking that a thousand copies would be ample, had destroyed the type—they could not imagine that a book which quoted the Bible could be a success—but in less than a month the whole edition was sold out and a new one demanded. Although criticism did not cease, Gide had become overnight an author who sold.

Except for *La Symphonie Pastorale*, conceived at the same time as *La Porte Étroite*, though only finished nine years later, and which he then called his last tribute to the past, Gide had finished expounding the problem of his married life. He wished now to emancipate himself from previous preoccupations, and he began to write *Corydon*, to set forth the problem of his homosexuality; by 1910 he had finished two dialogues of this apology —justification rather—of homosexuality, and even went so far as to have them privately printed, but he allowed himself to be dissuaded by his brother-in-law from publishing them. Instead he wrote *Isabelle*, which is the least personal of all his works and contains nothing of himself or of anyone closely connected with him, though it does take place in landscapes that he knew near his property La Roque. It is not an important work, though it shows mastery and skill, and some fine descriptive writing. It is a tale of mystery and murder, of shots in the dark, of adultery and an illegitimate crippled child. It is the subject of the 'roman noir', but with a Gidian twist that gives it originality. Isabelle, as she is on the point of eloping with her lover, is seized with panic at the thought of freedom, and she sends an old servant to intercept him and to prevent him reaching her; he is over-zealous and kills him. Through refusing to yield to temptation —a very Gidian conception—and through fear of liberty, Isabelle lost her chance of fulfilment and all in vain, for she later became no better than a whore. The story might have been the conventional one of a young girl seduced by her lover, but prevented from eloping with him by a faithful retainer, and then bearing a crippled child through her efforts to disguise her condition. That hers should be the real guilt adds spice to the story.

Isabelle closes the first part of Gide's main creative phase. In this period he began to write literary criticism, in which he is far from negligible. *Prétextes* was published in 1903 and was followed by *Nouveaux Prétextes* in 1911. Then too he began to collect a host of followers somewhat younger than himself, not the large number of the nineteen-twenties, but nevertheless a goodly number, most of whom counted in literature before the First World War. Amongst them were Ghéon, Copeau, Schlumberger, Rivière and many others. With some of them he founded *La Nouvelle Revue Française* in 1908, which continued until the Second World War to unite and to publish the most progressive writers in France.

V

If it die

Les Caves du Vatican marks the transition between the first and second parts of Gide's main creative period, and it indicates the break with the past. It was begun in October 1911 and finished in June 1913. In construction it is similar to the later work *Les Faux Monnayeurs*; in both novels the various plots are skilfully interwoven at different points to form a pattern of great complexity. In *Les Caves du Vatican* the points of intersection are formed by the fact that the main characters in this devious story, with all its plots and ramifications, are members of the same family, either by birth or marriage.

Gide calls it not a novel but a 'sotie' which, by dictionary definition, is a work in which everyone is mad or foolish. He wishes to show all the ways in which men are fools. Fools are those who live in a certain system of beliefs in order to attack those who live in another; fools are the 'bien pensants' with their bigoted faith; fools too the free-thinkers just as bigoted in their atheism; fools too the ambitious pursuing vain honours. All of them are fools afraid of life. Amongst them stands out the hero, Lafcadio, the free individual, a bastard bound by no ties to the past. He is a young man somewhat like the David in Gide's play *Saul*, but even more like Julien Sorel in Stendhal's novel *Le Rouge et le Noir*. He is a youth handsome and strong in body and determination who, whenever he considers that he has betrayed his real feelings, punishes himself by plunging a knife into his thigh. It is he who has the courage and daring to perform the 'acte gratuit' when he kills a complete stranger, one of the fools of the 'sotie' and a born victim.

Les Caves du Vatican ends on the question of whether or no Lafcadio is going to give himself up to the police for his crime. Gide liked this uncertain ending and was to use it again in *Les Faux Monnayeurs*. We must assume that Lafcadio did not die, since he was to be the hero of the later novel which was to be composed of his private diary. He was eventually to become Bernard in the finished work.

Les Caves du Vatican is an amusing and brilliantly written book the irony of which is more subtle than that of *Paludes* or *Le Prométhée mal enchaîné*. There are some critics who consider it as Gide's greatest and most accomplished work, though not all would agree with this opinion. There are many, on the contrary, who feel that he reaches greater heights when his work is inspired by deep human emotion, contained in and restrained by perfect language.

The work brought him much criticism from Catholics on account of its flippancy and anti-clericalism, and it made Gide's relations with Paul Claudel very strained. One of the reasons which inspired him to write it may well have been irritation against his friend who had been trying, since they met in 1905, not always tactfully, to convert him to Catholicism. The quarrel over *Les Caves du Vatican* virtually put an end to their friendship. Gide had borrowed a line from Claudel's play, *L'Annonce faite à Marie*, as a heading to the section dealing with the papal conspiracy, which said: 'Of what King speak you and of what Pope? For there are two and no one knows which is the true one'. Claudel was naturally referring to the fourteenth-century, when there were two claimants to the papacy, and he requested Gide to remove this line from his work as he did not wish to be connected with it in any way, both on account of its attitude to Catholicism and its very dubious moral tone.

There now occurred a psychological crisis in Gide's life which lasted for some years and from which he emerged a very different person. The crisis had started before he began *Les Caves du Vatican*, and as a result he went through years of deep mental suffering and turmoil. We can reconstruct the general lines from his correspondence with Claudel. It was an emotional as well as religious crisis—or rather it was an emotional conflict which gave rise to a religious one. Gide always needed some conflict in order to obtain the energy for composition. He wanted now to study the problem of his homosexuality. He felt that it should be eradicated or else accepted, not furtively, but openly. This problem had begun to trouble him after he had finished *La Porte Étroite* and it continued all through the writing of *Les Caves du Vatican*. He wished to complete his *Corydon* and to make full confession, in total sincerity. The conflict came to a head when Claudel requested Gide to remove the offending quotation from his book and then went on to say that he considered it dangerous for Gide from every point of view. He warned him that he ought to realise that after *Saul* and *L'Immoraliste* he should be very careful, and not place weapons in the hands of his opponents. He asked him how he could have written certain passages in the book and then said: 'Must we then believe, what I have never wished to, that you are yourself a participant in these hideous practices? Answer me you must! If you are not a homosexual, then why this strange predilection for that sort of subject? If you are one, then unfortunate man get treated and don't publish these abominations.'

This started a long and acrimonious argument. Gide answered heatedly demanding by what right his friend asked such questions in such a manner. He said that he made no mystery of his leanings and went on, in the strictest confidence, to confide in him his secret conflict, begging him not to reveal it to anyone. 'If I were alone', he said, 'I could make little of the contempt of the world, but I am a married man. As for the harm which you say my books are doing, I cannot believe it since I have come to realise the number of people whom the hypocrisy of our morals stifles as it does me . . . I cannot believe that religion casts out those who are like me. Through what cowardice, since God calls on me to speak, can I burke the question in my books? I have not chosen to be thus. I can struggle against my desires, I can overcome them, but I cannot choose the object of these desires nor invent others by imitation.' Then he confessed to him, as to a priest whose duty it was to keep his secret. 'I have never felt any desire towards a woman, and the great tragedy of my life is that the most constant and deep love is not, in my case, accompanied by what usually precedes it. It seems as if, on the contrary, love in me prevented desire.' He renewed his request for discretion: 'I implore you then to consider only this, that I love my wife more than my life, and that I could never forgive you if any act of yours touched her happiness'. He begged for his help and said: 'I do not know how to solve the problem which God has inscribed in my flesh'.

Claudel answered saying that God has not allowed anyone the right to use his own judgment to decide between right and wrong, that the law is written in black and white for all to follow. And moreover he considered that cynicism is worse than hypocrisy, that to sin and then to do penance is preferable to trying afterwards to find excuses and justifications. 'I repeat you are destroying yourself, putting yourself outside the pale, amongst those who are outside the pale, outside humanity. Public opinion in Paris hides itself better, but it is every bit as merciless as in London. You won't count any more.' He said that if Gide would remove the offensive paragraphs, little by little all would be forgotten. This was the most unbearable cut of all to Gide. 'Shall I confess that your striking phrase "little by little all will be forgotten" seems to me shameful', he answered. 'No! I do not want whitewash or compromise.'

In a desperate effort to obtain help in his struggle Gide now turned, for a time, towards the Catholic faith; and it was then that his friends hoped most for his conversion.

In the meantime the First Great War had broken out. In July 1914 Gide had been on the point of going to England; he had even bought his ticket and was about to embark at Dieppe when he bought a paper and suddenly realised that war was inevitable. He hurried back to Cuverville to look after his wife. When war finally came he went to Paris to find some work to help in the war effort. He thought at first that during a war a writer's duty was to abstain from writing. He worked in the early days for the Red Cross, and next in a convalescent home for soldiers. Then, with the German advance on Paris, he feared for the safety of his wife, and returned to Cuverville to arrange for the evacuation of the women and children of the village. He stood at his own door, waiting for the arrival of the enemy. Then came the Battle of the Marne, and the thrust towards the Channel ports was averted. In October 1914 he became assistant director of a Foyer Franco-Belge, to give food and shelter to the refugees. He remained there for nearly eighteen months and then, through some cabal, he was deposed from office and returned to Cuverville. He took up again his pre-war preoccupations and began once more to write and think.

His thoughts were much taken up with religious speculations, especially when a close friend was killed at the front; he was a recent convert to Catholicism and the moving letters which he wrote to his wife, and which Gide had read, broke down much of his lack of faith. There was also the conversion of Ghéon, in January 1916, which moved him greatly. The day after he heard of it he read the opening verses from the fifteenth chapter of Saint John, and they assumed for him an added meaning. 'If a man abide not in me, he is cast forth as a branch and is withered; and men gather them and cast them into the fire; and they are burnt.' He felt suddenly that he himself had been cast into the fire, the fire of abominable desires. He suddenly saw that everything in him needed reforming and that he must conquer his sensuality. Seeking help in his struggle, he thought he might find it in religion. All through 1916 he dwelt in darkness and distress of soul. In February he began to keep two diaries, the usual one in which he recorded his daily life, and another, published later under the title *Numquid et tu*, in which he related his anguished search for God.

George Painter, in his recent biography, sees the conflict differently. He explains it as due merely to a conventional emotional triangle when, according to him, Gide fell in love with the daughter of his eldest woman friend, a girl young enough to be his daughter, and sought help from this in religion. He does not give his evidence for this statement, and Gide's *Journal* and letters do not support it. Moreover Gide assured Claudel that he had never felt desire for any woman, and in his posthumous work, *Nunc manet in Te*, he declared that he was capable of sexual power only when his emotions were not involved.

There was, however, certainly some serious difference between Gide and his wife during 1916, for he did not write in his *Journal* for three months and said afterwards: 'I take up this *Journal* again which I dropped last June. I had torn up all the last pages for they reflected a terrible crisis in which Em was involved, or more exactly of which she was the cause.' Since these pages had been written for her he destroyed them as soon as she had read them, if not exactly at her request, because he knew that that was what she would have wished. However, he later regretted them bitterly because he said that they were amongst the most heart-felt he had ever written.

This new love for another woman—if love there really was—remains mysterious, for Gide does not speak of it, and it did not in any way impair his deep devotion for his wife. In October 1916 there was some plan that he should spend the winter with old friends in the south of France, but when he spoke of it to Madeleine, he saw such resigned sadness on her face that he abandoned all thought of the visit. He gave it up, he said, as well as many other projects, because anything which he would have purchased at the expense of her happiness would no longer have brought him pleasure.

La Symphonie Pastorale was finished after the mental tribulations of this year. Painter believes that what he calls the love affair with the young woman coloured his view of the novel (which had been conceived in 1910) and altered it.

La Symphonie Pastorale is a return to the novel in the first person, and it consists of the diary kept by a Swiss Protestant minister who is, as was Michel in *L'Immoraliste*, what Gide feared that he might become if he gave way to certain of his tendencies. Although he shares many of the minister's characteristics, he is not wholly like him, and he was much annoyed when people tried to identify him with him. It is, as are most of Gide's books, a work of criticism. He criticizes the materialistic attitude to religion of the wife, but also the way in which the minister manages to deceive himself and to twist the Gospels to suit his own ends. It is Gide's most despairing work, and evil seems to be triumphant all along the line. Although it has certain faults of construction, especially a very faulty ending, it is a work of great beauty and purity. The style is more effortless than even in *La Porte Étroite*, and more stripped of lyricism and imagery; it is Racinian in its telling economy, which matches the purity of the landscape and the religious nature of the subject. All the characters are well drawn and the minister is one of Gide's most masterly creations, one of the best portraits of the hypocrite, or rather self-deceiver, in French literature.

After the book was published Gide tells us that he received a letter expressing surprise that he could have written such a work after *Les Caves du Vatican* and that he answered that it was a debt to the past which he had not settled and which was now liquidated. He means that it belonged to the individual problems which he had treated in *L'Immoraliste* and *La Porte Étroite*. He had now finished with that phase of his life forever.

When Gide started his religious Journal, *Numquid et tu*, in which he set down his anguished search for belief, he was willing to sacrifice his personal liberty for the comfort and support of complete faith. However, no matter how long and how earnestly he prayed, grace did not descend on him; his spiritual pride was too great and he did not recover the heart of a child as he had hoped. When the conflict was over he left revealed religion behind him forever, though he never lost his longing for God. 'Catholicism is inadmissible', he said, 'protestantism is intolerable; and I feel profoundly Christian'.

1916 had been a year of great distress and perplexity for him, but when it ended he reached calmer waters. He solved to his satisfaction the problem of his homosexuality. Its solution was helped by his relationship with Marc, which began in 1917. In spite of all that has been written about Gide's homosexuality this is the only known relationship of this kind, the only one that was more than a furtive encounter.

Then Gide decided to turn his back on his past and to be moral in his own way. He cast aside self-torture, hair-splitting about motives and guilt, and became what he thought was finally himself. 'I allow the contradictions to live in me.'

Then, wishing to liquidate the past and to start afresh, he planned his autobiography, *Si le Grain ne meurt*, meaning to indicate by the title that except the seed die it cannot bring forth fruit. The seeds that will bring forth much fruit in the harvest to come will be the seeds of his dead past, all the distress and 'angst' of his earlier years. He wanted them to die now so that he could begin a new life of freedom and serenity. He began writing it in 1916, though the greater part of it was written after the War. It was first privately printed in 1920 and 1921, but the commercial edition appeared only in 1926. It is an .ccount of his life from his birth to his marriage. Here is again recorded his love for his cousin, the 'mystic orientation' of his life. It ranks amongst the great autobiographies of the world, though it is nearer in form to confessions. It has not the abundance of Rousseau's *Confessions*, nor their lyric sweep, but it has a classic restraint that makes it worthy of the great masters of French prose in the seventeenth century. It contains passages of Gide's finest writing, although it has frequently been severely attacked for its frankness and its discussion of homosexuality.

In May 1917 Gide began his long and deep attachment for Marc, the son of an old friend. It was the friendship in his life which brought him most joy, for a number of years at all events, and was the main reason for his recovery at the end of the War. He adopted him as a son and took him over to England when he went there in June 1918. This overt action of Gide's wounded his wife more deeply than anything she had yet endured with him. We do not know what she said to him—it was not her habit to say much—but he wrote in his *Journal*: 'I leave France in an indescribable state of anguish. It seems to me that I am saying farewell to the whole of my past.'

When he returned home again he had occasion to ask to see the letters he had written to Madeleine since his boyhood—perhaps he needed some material for his autobiography. Then she confessed to him that after he had had gone to England she had burnt them. He was shattered at this unexpected blow from her who had always been so gentle, that she should do this to him. He knew that he had always put the best of himself in his letters to her, and it was as if she had killed their child, his and hers, when she had destroyed them. He wept for over a week, from morning till night, near the fireside, in the living-room with her, and at night alone in his room, hoping against hope that she would come to him, that she would make some sign. That was the bitterest blow of all, her indifference. She went about the little daily jobs, never looking his way. He felt that he had lost her, that everything was shattered in him, the past, the present and the future. He hoped for days that she would yield and come, but she went about the daily round passing beside him as if she did not see him. He did not recover his confidence in life until many years had passed and he felt that he had regained once more her esteem. Seven years later he wrote: 'Since then I have lived only, as it were, a kind of posthumous life, on the fringe of real life.'

The second part of *Si le Grain ne meurt* was written after the destruction of the letters.

She too, poor woman, must have suffered deeply when she found herself alone in the great house, after he had gone to England with Marc; and then, in a panic of despair, she destroyed the letters. Yet they were, she once admitted, her most precious possession; but seeing him have so little regard for her, in her humility, she doubted his love for her and would keep nothing of him, no reminder.

For almost twenty years she lived estranged from him, making all efforts to detach herself, to destroy everything that might still attach him. She now gave to God what she had once given to him, and he was jealous of this rival who was stealing everything that he longed to have. In *Nunc manet in te* he expresses his distress as he sees her turning more and more not to the protestantism of her upbringing but to the Catholicism of her forbears. One of her friends has said, since her death, that it was only loyalty to Gide that prevented her final conversion.

Yet, in spite of everything, Gide knew that he loved her more deeply and more desperately than ever. In 1925, when he was leaving for Africa, he begged a friend to tell her, should he not return, that she had always remained his dearest and most precious treasure, and that it was because he loved her more than life itself, that, since she had withdrawn from him, life seemed to him of so small price.

VI

The Counterfeiters

A great change came over Gide as he emerged from the crisis of the War years. He grew less anxious and his face began to assume the expression which surprised those who knew him first in the nineteen-twenties. In 1928 he wrote to Charles du Bos: 'It is true that I have ceased to love "angst". I think it is good to have known it, but that it is wrong to remain in it and to love it for itself. That is why Pascal touches me nowadays less than Goethe.'

He next finished *Corydon*, which had been hanging fire for so many years that he had feared lest someone should forestall him, for he considered it a topic of such urgent interest that anyone might wish to treat it. He finished it in June 1918 but, restrained by his friends, he still hesitated to publish it.

In the meantime his next published work was one dealing with Dostoevsky, composed of talks which he gave at the Vieux Colombier in 1922 to celebrate the centenary of Dostoevsky's birth. It marks an important stage in Gide's development as a writer, for it reflects the moment when he was emerging from the state of the tormented introvert whom we knew in the early works, and becoming the serene philosopher of the later years. Here, for the first time, he suggests that happiness may well come from renunciation, and that the individual may triumph by sacrificing his individualism; or, as he was later to say: 'the triumph of the individual is in renouncing individualism'. Dostoevsky showed him that he who lives cherishing his own life shall lose it, and that he who surrenders it shall earn life eternal. Gide was now moving towards altruism and forgetfulness of self. He saw in Dostoevsky the reconciliation of extremes, a man who accepted his inconsistencies and proved that the imploring cry of anguished humanity could never rise from the righteous who are sure of their own salvation. Gide contrasts his psychological portrayal with that of Corneille, who depicts characters trying to conform with an ideal which makes them different from what nature intended them to be if they yielded to their natural impulses.

Although, in these lectures, Gide was trying to be objective, it was still himself that he was unconsciously seeking; and he discovered in Dostoevsky only what was like himself, what would be useful to himself.

Eventually, in 1924, Gide determined to publish *Corydon*. It was probably Proust's sorry picture of inversion in *Sodome et Gomorrhe*, published in 1923, that finally urged him to action. He was disgusted that Proust had exemplified only the ugly and decrepit aspect of homosexuality, and had never shown it young and fair. He stigmatised his attitude as hypocritical and cowardly, for Proust had admitted to him that the fairer aspects had been used to embellish heterosexual love in *A l'Ombre des Jeunes Filles en Fleur*.

To the end of his life Gide considered *Corydon* as one of his most important works, but most readers find its special pleading unconvincing. It takes the form of Socratic dialogues. The narrator is a militant heterosexual who has been much perturbed by certain homosexual scandals. He calls on Corydon, a doctor of medicine and also a well-known homosexual, to discuss the matter with him so that he can arrive at an unprejudiced opinion. Corydon argues with his friend, and proves to his complete satisfaction, by zoology first, that homosexuality is not contrary to nature; next by sociology that the only reason why heterosexuality prevails is that it is favoured by convention and training; and finally he goes to history to establish that the epochs when homosexuality was most rife—in classical Greece and during the Renaissance—were epochs of rich artistic, intellectual and spiritual achievement, and that, on the contrary, the prevalence of heterosexual love is a symptom of decadence.

The result is a cold and logical argument the premises of which cannot be accepted, and this alienates sympathy. This was a deliberate purpose as Gide explains, saying that he had avoided all arguments which would touch the heart as he wanted to appeal only to the head.

The publishing of *Corydon* was disastrous to Gide in every way. He was violently attacked on all sides, even by close friends, many of whom he lost. His wife was very much distressed by the unsavoury publicity it aroused and she wrote to him: 'What disturbs me is the evil campaign which has been started against you. Ah! if you were invulnerable I shouldn't be so much afraid. But you are vulnerable and you know it and I know it.' She defied him to find a single honest person who approved of the book; but then, as Gide remarked, she would not consider anyone who did approve of it an honest man.

Gide was startled and amazed at what he considered an unforeseen betrayal. He sold his house in Paris and all his books

41

—even those inscribed to him by writers who were his friends. In the Preface to the catalogue of the sale he wrote :'Since he [that is himself] is planning a long absence, he has decided to part with his books amongst which are those which had remained very dear to him so long as they awakened only memories of friendship'.

Gide was to leave Paris as soon as he had finished *Les Faux Monnayeurs* on which he was working. He completed it in June 1925, and then set out for French equatorial Africa whence he was to return only a year later.

In *Les Faux Monnayeurs* we have something different from Gide's previous works. He calls it his only novel, meaning to indicate that the canvas is larger than in his previous tales, where the characters are limited almost to the main protagonists. It is true that the frame-work of *Les Caves du Vatican* is almost as large, but that is a 'sotie' and not a novel.

In *Les Faux Monnayeurs* he would have liked to have been able to dispense with a plot—the ambition of all those who study man's nature deeply—and to include everything without limitation. Although there are some elements of himself in the novelist Edouard, the main character, he did not intend him to be a selfportrait; he makes it clear in *Le Journal des Faux Monnayeurs* that Edouard would never have been capable of achieving what he himself had done. He is, he claims, an amateur, a failure, a 'raté'. As there are so few elements of self-portrayal *Les Faux Monnayeurs* is the least subjective of his works, the most impersonal. It is a very deliberate composition, and he tells us that he aimed at achieving what Bach had done in *The Art of Fugue*, and that he did not see why what is possible in music should be impossible in literature. It is indeed a musical work in which the themes appear and disappear as in a fugue, and all the plots are interwoven with subtle musical skill. It is also a very complicated work, not easy to take in at a first reading; but if persevered with it becomes rewarding. The reader must visualise each character as belonging to several groups, sometimes playing a part in several actions at once. The main character, the novelist, is involved in all the actions and he is, musically speaking, the main subject, the main theme. It is he who draws all the subsidiary characters together. These, more complicated, subtle and tortuous than any hitherto in Gide's work, are all metaphorically counterfeiters—though only Strouvilhou and his associates are counterfeiters in the real sense —for each of them, as soon as he is with other people, even the children, acts a part and ceases to be himself. They all use the false coin of ready-made feelings. Only Bernard tries to find out what he is and to be simply and courageously himself. He is a further reincarnation of Lafcadio from *Les Caves du Vatican*, but Lafcadio grown noble and serious. Gide had first intended *Les Faux Monnayeurs* to be a continuation of *Les Caves du Vatican*, a further chapter in the history of its hero; and in the earliest drafts the character which eventually becomes Bernard was called Lafcadio. However, as Gide wrote, the characters developed out of his control and Bernard became a deeper and more interesting person than ever Lafcadio could have been. He, the finest character in the novel, wrestles with the angel who is also at times the devil, and comes out victorious. He decides on his future conduct, taking his formula from the novelist: 'One must follow one's bent, so long as it is upwards'. He should really have been the hero of the novel, but Gide grew to like Olivier so much that he could not bear to make another young man the hero, and so brought in the novelist to be the main character. Edouard, like Gide, is writing a novel which he is also going to call *Les Faux Monnayeurs*. We hear much of the difficulties he encounters, and this helps the reader to an understanding of Gide's problems of composition and his manner of solving them.

All Gide's well-known themes appear in *Les Faux Monnayeurs*: The conflict between youth and age; the struggle against conventions; the folly of those who live by too rigid principles; the urgent necessity of discovering one's true self; and so forth.

We find here too, for the first time, that altruism and wide sweeping human compassion which will be characteristic of Gide's next phase. The angel, with whom Bernard had struggled, leads him first to the grand Boulevards frequented by the rich full of self-confidence and unconscious of anyone but themselves, yet full of heavy cares. 'Is this happiness?' Bernard asks and feels his heart full of tears. The angel then leads him to the poorer quarters of the city and night begins to fall. They wander through the sordid streets where prostitution, crime, hunger and want lurk. Then Bernard grasps the hand of the angel who turns his face away to weep. The angel symbolises devotion to something beyond oneself.

Les Faux Monnayeurs is a *tour de force* in a very difficult and complicated technique, and it does not quite come off. This is largely because the separate themes are treated more slightly than is necessary, though to treat them fully would have required a novel of unprecedented length. Roger Martin du Gard felt the inadequacy of treatment, and he kept urging Gide to elaborate more fully. He tells us that there were to have been further chapters at the end, but that Gide, somewhat appalled at the thought of the work still needed to complete the novel, was very much relieved and proud when the idea occurred to end it on an interrogation which had no finality. Edouard says: 'I am curious to get to know Caloub'. Caloub is Bernard's young brother who has played no part in the novel, and we imagine it beginning all over again from a different angle; but Edouard has not finished his own *Faux Monnayeurs*, and we know that he will never complete it however many instalments he were given.

Gide himself does not seem to have thought that his novel was an unqualified success as it stood, for he published separately, under the title *Journal des Faux Monnayeurs*, the diary which he had kept while writing the book, and this is of immense interest and elucidates much that is not clear in the novel itself.

Les Faux Monnayeurs is an interesting and subtle work which has influenced the form of the novel all over the world, but it is not without serious faults of construction. The intervention of the author himself, such as occurs in the chapter entitled *The Author judges his Characters*, is out of place in a novel in the first person. There is in any case, without this aside, sufficient objective analysis of the characters. Indeed there is too much *Journal* altogether, and it seems too easy a way out of the difficulties of construction. Gide keeps a *Journal* while writing a novel; his hero is a novelist who also keeps a Journal while writing his own novel about a novelist who keeps a *Journal* while writing a further novel. It is as if one were looking at oneself in a mirror reflected in another mirror and so on to infinity.

When Gide set off for Africa in July 1925, Claudel thought that it was in defeat, with the deliberate intention of not returning—just as in old-fashioned English novels the jilted hero goes East to shoot big game. Then, with the tactlessness which was characteristic of him, he wrote to Madeleine Gide with the purpose of meeting her to discuss the problem of her husband, the outcast: 'Madame', he wrote, 'the impression obsesses me that perhaps you would like to discuss with me a being who is dear to you, whose thought has preoccupied me for twenty-five years, and whose key God has placed in your hands. If I am mistaken please forgive me. If not I should be happy to meet you where and when you like, either in Paris or Cuverville.' Her answer too is characteristic, characteristic of the woman whom Gide had loved so long and so devotedly. 'Dear Monsieur Claudel', she answered, 'your letter is for me a further pledge of the faithful friendship in God which you cherish for my husband. This friendship has always deeply touched me. I have felt, it is true, much anxiety concerning this long and distant visit to darkest Africa which he has wished—but if I had more faith, then I would not be so troubled. All those who love André Gide as that very noble soul deserves to be loved, must pray for him. I do it every day—and you also, don't you? It is thus, I think, that for his greatest good, we can best meet. Dear Monsieur, may I express to the friend that you are all my gratitude, and to the author my admiration.'

Gide, however, did not set out for Africa in any spirit of defeat, or to die there. He now emerged from distress and despair. The birth of his daughter in February 1923 gave him further reasons for hope in the future. She, like his favourite characters, was illegitimate, and he did not openly recognise her until the death of his wife in 1938. He hoped that his wife did not guess the truth, and he told Claude Mauriac that he had suffered much on that score, as he was never sure whether she

44

knew or not. Although she may not have known the girl's paternity, she did express disapproval of her illegitimate birth, and said that it was all due to the fact that her mother had been brought up without any religious principles. Painter says that in 1922 the love-affair of 1916 was resumed, but Gide's novel *Geneviève* would suggest the possibility of another interpretation. What is certain is that he was extremely proud of having produced a child, and was always delighted in pointing out to friends how like him she was, and how unmistakably his offspring. It was as if it were a constant marvel to him, to have fathered a child.

Gide set off for equatorial Africa with his young friend Marc, now a young man of twenty-three, who, on the journey, began to show his talent as a photographer by making an excellent film of the scenery and native life of Africa. In the thirties he was to produce exquisite films like *Lac aux Dames*.

Gide brought back from his travels two books, *Voyage au Congo* and *Retour du Tchad*. They are composed of the *Journal* that he kept during the trip, and contain descriptions of scenery, village dances, receptions by native chiefs. The amazed enchantment he had enjoyed when he was young returned to him and he forgot his age and the distress of his estrangement from his wife; he became young again. There are passages which might have come from *Les Nourritures Terrestres*, and foreshadow *Les Nouvelles Nourritures Terrestres* which was to appear ten years later. There is a moving little story which he extracted from the books and printed separately under the title *Dindiki*, the account of the death of his pet potto sloth who rode for hundreds of miles on his shoulder. The poor little beast suffered from some form of persistent constipation for which Gide tried every kind of cure, every kind of diet, in an endeavour to save it, and when it finally died he declared that he knew the sorrows of a bereaved parent.

VII

The God that failed

The journey to Africa cured Gide; and with his liberation from personal conflict he now felt free from his obsession of self, and had energy to spare for objective considerations, not merely for the problem of personal guilt and salvation. Freedom from the problem of self kindled in him a sense of social injustice which was to dominate his life for more than a decade. When he returned from Africa he wrote: 'Henceforth an immense lamentation dwells in me!' Then he said to Charles du Bos: 'I would like not only to reach happiness myself, but to make others reach it as well. I consider that it is in renouncing oneself. That is why to be happy is nothing; happiness is to make others

45

happy.' He now became the champion of under-dogs and victims—criminal offenders for whom he demanded more sympathetic treatment; women, for whom he asked equality —especially spiritual equality; and the colonial natives whose cause he pleaded in the two books he wrote on his return from Africa; and finally the socially under-privileged—it was then he took up Communism and went to Russia.

Gide's books about Africa created some sensation and there were even questions asked in parliament concerning the conditions which he described, but the Minister for the Colonies, in the usual manner of ministers, answered that everything would be put right in time.

The next works which he wrote were three novels forming a trilogy—*L'École des Femmes*, *Robert* and *Geneviève*—and they were undertaken to ask the question of what woman can expect in a modern world. The narrator of the first is Eveline, a woman who is in the period of 'décristallisation', as Stendhal might say. She had once loved her husband but has become disillusioned. He is an unconscious hypocrite who deceives himself about his true feelings and motives. *Robert* is the answer, in the first person, by the husband, and very cleverly Gide makes him convict himself out of his own mouth. Here the portrait of the hypocrite is deepened. Six months after finishing *Robert* Gide began the third volume of the trilogy, *Geneviève*, which was to tell the story from the point of view of the younger generation, the daughter of Eveline, the modern girl of the nineteen-twenties, but he was to find it impossible to finish for many years. At first he intended his heroine to reach salvation through Communism, but after he had worked on the novel for a couple of years, he saw the artistic mistake of using a character in a creative work as a vehicle for his personal opinions. He thought then of writing an abstract work on Communism; this was however never written, as he became disillusioned before he could do so; and he purged *Geneviève* of political theorising. The novel was rewritten several times during the next few years, and finally, despairing of ever finding a satisfactory solution, he published the two parts which were already written, and never wrote any more.

Gide felt that the problem he had chosen was incapable of solution, that Nature had weighted the scales too heavily against woman, not on the physical plane alone which is the only aspect usually considered, but on the spiritual and emotional plane as well. The real enslaver of woman is her own temperament. Geneviève says to her mother: 'I cannot admit to give myself entirely to someone', and Eveline replies: 'You speak as someone who has never loved'.

The trilogy is written in Gide's most austere style, when he had stripped it of all ornamentation and metaphor, in an effort, as he said, to reach the classicism of Racine's art without sacrificing any of the poetry. He declared that ornamentation

46

served merely to conceal faults and blemishes, and that only a thought which was not sufficiently beautiful need fear complete nakedness. Some readers, however, have found the style of the trilogy too stark and unrelieved, and indeed it does not always avoid aridity and monotony; but, at its best, it has a deceptive simplicity and austerity which only a supreme artist could achieve.

There now emerges a new shade in Gide's conception of liberty. In his play *Oedipe*, of 1931, the hero exemplifies the final and utter destruction which comes to the individual when he accepts nothing as greater than himself, and values his personal liberty above all else. Yet Oedipus starts out with all the advantages which Gide thinks necessary for a free individual, but is finally defeated by trying to be completely self-sufficient.

Oedipus, King of Thebes, discovers that the man he has killed in self-defence is his father, and that the woman he has married is his mother. He blinds himself in retribution and goes into exile. It is a punishment for his past egoism and spiritual blindness, and he now accepts a new discipline. He becomes convinced that man without God is doomed to defeat and despair unless he substitutes another idea for that of God. Oedipus rejects the God he has once adored, and chooses man; Gide took up Communism. He now thought that liberty was not sufficient in itself, that it destroyed itself if it was not linked to some ideal beyond mere egoistic self-expression—to some duty even. In 1931 he wrote in a preface to *Vol de Nuit*, by Antoine de Saint Exupéry: 'I am particularly grateful to him for having thrown light on that paradoxical truth, which is of paramount importance, that the happiness of man does not lie in liberty but in the acceptance of some duty'. He now talked of 'l'individualisme serviable mais non servile'. This is a new departure from the individualistic and personal sense of liberty expressed thirty years before. Looking then for some duty, some sense of obligation and responsibility, he turned to Communism. He thought that he would find there, with its ideal of service, with its discipline, the complete affirmation of the individual. 'The triumph of the individual', he wrote then, 'is in renouncing individualism'. He declared that for a long time, for too long a time, he had been without a *credo*, but that he had finally found faith, and that was in the belief in the future of the Soviet Union. Hitherto he had had the reputation of being a man who would not commit himself, but now he committed himself whole-heartedly and uncompromisingly to the Communist solution for the ills of the world, and it was a kind of religious conversion. In 1931 he wrote: 'I would like to cry aloud my sympathy for the Soviet Union, and hope that my cry might be heard and have effect. I would like to live long enough to witness the triumph of that tremendous effort, which I hope from the bottom of my heart will succeed, and for which I would like to work.' Although he was ready to sacrifice some

47

of the sanctity of his individuality, he did not think that this should be necessary, or that there was any reason why there should be a clash between individualism and Communism.

It was not through Marx but through the Gospels that Gide reached Communism, and in 1932 he wrote: 'My conversion is like a faith. My whole being is bent towards one single goal, all my thoughts—even involuntary—lead me back to it. In the deplorable state of distress of the modern world, the plan of the Soviet Union seems to me to point to salvation. Everything persuades me of this. And if my life were necessary to assure the success of the Soviet Union, I would gladly give it immediately. I write this with a cool and calm head, in full sincerity, through great need to leave at least this testimony, in case death should intervene before I have time to express myself better.'

In 1935 Gide produced the only major work which appeared during his Communistic period, *Les Nouvelles Nourritures Terrestres*, addressed to the same Nathanael as the first *Nourritures Terrestres*. He had already published a fragment of it in 1921, composed just after he had emerged from his Season in Hell, and when he was in the early days of his relationship with Marc. The greater part of Book One was written in an ecstasy of joy in life. But soon there came the tragic contrast in a series of passages entitled *Rencontres*, describing Baudelairean characters —outcasts and failures—encountered in the streets of Paris. Nathanael asks him the reason for these tales of sadness in a book dedicated to joy, and he answers that he does not want happiness that springs from another's sorrow, and that, in order to be happy himself, he needs the happiness of others. He adds that there are in the world such immensities of poverty, distress and grief that a man of integrity cannot be happy, for he sees them. He declares that his reason cannot hold him back on the slope of Communism which seems to him to lead upwards, but, on the contrary, has joined his heart there. He now addresses Nathanael as 'comrade' and says that progress is only possible by thrusting aside the past; he cites the example of Lot's wife who was turned into a pillar of salt, a pillar of frozen tears, because she had looked behind.

During a meeting in Paris of *L'Union pour la Vérité* in 1935, when Gide was asked to defend his opinions, he answered: 'I consider that on account of its compromises Christianity is bankrupt. I have written, and I firmly believe, that if Christianity had really prevailed, and if it had fulfilled the teaching of Christ, there would be today no question of Communism, there would indeed be no social problem at all.' He added later, during the general discussion: 'If I have felt no contradiction between the community and its individual position, it is precisely because that contradiction is only theoretical and artificial. It is not Marx who brought me to Communism—I have made the most strenuous efforts to read him, but in vain. I persevere, but it is certainly not his theory that won me over. What

rought me to Communism, with my whole heart, was the fact
f the privileged position which I personally enjoy—that seemed
o me preposterous and intolerable.' He had become ashamed
f being a man of independent means, of never having been
bliged to earn his bread in the sweat of his brow.

Many people, however, amongst them his colleagues of the
Nouvelle Revue Française, thought that he was speaking without
ufficient experience or knowledge of the Soviet Union, and
ean Schlumberger, in a leading article, advised him that he
ught to go there and see it all at first hand. So, in June 1936,
ide took up the challenge, and went to Russia, with three
ther writers, all as guests of the Soviet Government.

He went to Russia hoping that the Soviet Union would be
ble to produce the finest flowers of civilization without en-
laving the mind, or reducing to serfdom a single class, or
enying the benefits of civilization to anyone. He went to
ussia fully realising that a new world might entail sacrifice of
uch that was good in itself; he knew that some artistic stand-
rds might have to be lowered for a time, for the sake of social
nd material gain. He agreed that men could not be improved
orally and intellectually until the social abuses had been re-
oved, and the social system altered. He was eventually to
onsider that the price it entailed was too high. He could then
iscover no difference between what he saw in huge letters on
he walls of Italy and what he observed in Russia. There were
he same slogans, 'Believe, obey and fight', identical in both
reeds. The Communist spirit had ceased to be contrary to the
ascist spirit, or even differing from it.

Gide reached Communism through the Gospels, but he found
ittle of that spirit in Russia itself. He was fêted everywhere,
or he was a glorious gain, the greatest living European writer
nd a man known for his integrity and fairness of mind. He had
howered on him all the privileges of a decadent civilization;
ut he did not need incense, for he was singularly free from per-
onal vanity. He saw everywhere the gulf which separates the
rivileged from the underprivileged; the same enslavement of
he mind against which he had protested elsewhere. He had
one to the Soviet Union to find criticism allied to discipline,
 new conception of life and liberty. 'No culture is possible with-
ut criticism', he said; but in Russia he found no possibility of
oubt or criticism.

Gide had set out for Russia in June 1936 full of hopes; his
ubsequent disillusionment is expressed in the two books which
e wrote on his return, *Retour de l'U.R.S.S.* and *Retouches à mon
Retour de l'U.R.S.S.* One cannot claim that these books are
mongst Gide's most satisfactory, intellectually or artistically,
ut much of what was considered prejudice in 1936 is seen now
s sound judgment.

When Gide had finished these books he said that they were
he final payment in the long sacrifice that he had made of his

art to social preoccupations. 'Since these began to encumbe my head and my heart', he said, 'I have written nothing o value'. That is true, and the thirties are Gide's leanest years a far as literary productions are concerned. During the Secon World War, looking back on that period, he said: 'Slowly came to convince myself that when I thought I was a Commu nist, I was in fact a Christian'.

Between the entries for April and August 1938 a thick blac line is ruled across the pages of Gide's *Journal*. This symbol c mourning marks the death of Madeleine Gide. He was, sadly not with her when she died. A telegram from Cuverville re called him from where he was staying. He was, as he says, witl a woman of his acquaintance, but he does not give her name The prodigal arrived too late on this final occasion. He hac left his wife a few days earlier in a 'precarious state of health' but not in an alarming one, so that he departed without fear 'She was not only what I loved most in the world', he wrot at her death-bed, on his return, 'but it even seemed to me tha it was in relation to her that I lived'. As he gazed on her, lyin ready for burial, he reflected that there was now in her fac none of that smiling amenity which, in life, had always tempered her gravity. She seemed like Alissa from *La Porte Étroite* who likewise, had died alone. She resembled one of the Jansenist painted by Philippe de Champagne.

Happily, at the end, after their estrangement of almost twent years, they drew near one another again. It was when she feared for his safety during his ill-fated visit to Russia. This nev closeness *in extremis* was amongst the sweetest experiences that h had known with her. She allowed him then to do things for he permitted to no one else; to dress the ulcers on her legs, aban doning herself gratefully to his care, and was nearer to him ther than at any other time since their marriage; so that old anc infirm as she was he felt that he loved her more than ever. Afte fifty years the mystic orientation of his life remained the same

It was of her that he had written, five years before she died when she was sixty-six: 'Each time that I see her again I fee anew that I have never really loved but her; and it even seem to me that I love her more than ever'.

The pages of his *Journal* in which after her death he record his distress and despair, so that, as he says, another in simila circumstances may on reading feel less alone, are amongst the most poignant that he ever wrote.

He was now free, free as he had never been before, he though ironically, but it was only the freedom of a kite when the strinş is cut. He spent the summer of 1938 at Cuverville, where En had always lived, and to which the prodigal had so often re turned, trying to find reasons for continuing to live. 'Since sh is there no more', he wrote, 'I have only pretended to live without taking any interest in anything, or in myself; withou appetite, without taste, with neither curiosity nor desire, anc in a disillusioned universe; with hope for nothing else save to leave it'.

He realised, however, that if he did not find serenity, then his life would have been in vain. 'If I do not manage to reach serenity then my whole philosophy is bankrupt'.

The last line in the collected volume of his *Journal*, before the War, is an adaptation of the final words from *Le Cimetière Marin* by Paul Valéry: 'Il faut tenter de vivre'. Gide says: 'Here am I free, as I have been before; terribly free. Shall I still have power to "tenter de vivre"?'

VIII

The Testament of Theseus

Gide was almost seventy when the Second World War broke out. His first reaction was one of horror—not only for France, but for the whole of civilization which might perish. It was when it was threatened that he began to realise fully the greatness of the works it had produced. It was then that he began to see the value of tradition and to appreciate the past. During the winter of the 'phony war' it was classical authors that he read, as if to cling to them before they were carried away by the hurricane of war—Racine and La Fontaine—passages of which he learned by heart so that they could never be taken from him. La Fontaine especially kept his thoughts from dwelling on the disasters of war. 'Ah! how, with him, we are far from the war', he wrote.

Then came the defeat of 1940, which he accepted, refusing all excuses—it was as if it were a personal defeat which he acknowledged, and for which he took full blame. He was enraged by the articles of explanation and excuses which the newspapers published. He agreed with Pétain when, in his first speech, just before the Armistice, he said: 'Since the victory [that is of 1918] the spirit of enjoyment has conquered the spirit of sacrifice. They wanted to economise effort and today they are reaping disaster.' A few days later he heard with stupour the Marshal's second address when he denounced the Free French and England. Gide imagined, in exculpation, that his speech might have been dictated to him by the Germans. 'Is it not enough that France should be vanquished, must she also be dishonoured?' That dishonour he thought the cruellest of France's defeats.

In August 1940 he wrote that the philosophic acceptance of fate—the *Amor Fati* of Nietzsche—did not go as far as the acceptance of the disaster. This explains the horror that he felt in 1941 when he received Chardonne's book, *Chronique Privée de l'An 1940*. Yet Chardonne had been a writer whom he had formerly admired and encouraged; but he could not accept, from a

Frenchman, his idealisation of the German defeat of France, nor the plea, pretending to come from the French point of view, in favour of German domination in Europe. Chardonne declared that he wished to view the present with the impartiality of a future historian. He said that historic events are always obscure for those who are living through them, and generally horrible. Only very much later will they be fully explained and then they will prove to have been beneficial. In this manner he was able to make out a good case for the disaster which had overwhelmed France—it was an event of history, like the defeat of the Roman Empire.

During 1941 and 1942 Gide published in *Le Figaro* a series of imaginary interviews, in which he showed that he had completely regained the verve and irony which he had temporarily lost since the death of his wife. It is the same style of brilliant satire which he had used in *Paludes*, but inspired now by the serenity and courage of an old man who had been able to encompass events intellectually. His sword had not lost its sleight nor his tongue its cunning. The interviews were supposed to deal with innocent literary topics—grammar, prosody, the novel and the future of poetry. But there is some brilliant *double entendre* when dealing subtly with the contrast between the genuine French spirit and the cowardly treachery of Vichy. The values which Gide postulates are those which we have met frequently before in his work—indeed he says that he must resign himself to repeat himself if he is not to talk arrant nonsense.

In these interviews a further development in Gide's conception of individuality and liberty becomes apparent, a new departure from the total and irresponsible liberty of his youth, and also from the 'liberté serviable' of his middle years. Now he believes that absolute liberty destroys the individual, and also society, unless it be closely linked with tradition and discipline. He declares that if civilization depended solely on those who initiated the revolutionary theories, then it would perish, since culture needs, for its survival, a continuous and developing tradition. Yet he had claimed earlier that the world could only advance on the dead bodies of those who went before, on the dead ideas of those who had preceded us. Now he believes in preserving our heritage, our Graeco-Roman heritage based on Christian principles—Gide never strayed far from the Gospels.

For two years after the fall of France Gide remained in the south of France with his daughter, either with his friends Madame Van Rysselberghe and her daughter, or else with Simon and Dorothy Bussy. Finally, in May 1942, he sailed for North Africa and there he spent the rest of the War. When it was liberated he could have gone over to England—a plane was ready to take him—but he preferred to remain with his own people. He founded a new literary magazine, *L'Arche*, the title of which explains itself, to take the place of *La Nouvelle Revue Française* which had collaborated with the Germans.

There, in North Africa, in the clear white light of Tunis, he thought again of the myth which had followed him through most of his life, the myth of Theseus, the builder of Athens. There it came to life and he began to write it. It was published in 1946 and it is his last great work, his literary testament.

The theme of Theseus had dwelt with him now for almost half a century. It is interesting to see how it has developed and altered during these years. At first he saw the thread which bound Theseus to Ariadne as a hindrance, dragging him back to whence he had come, to woman, who will always be a brake on man's desire for progress. This was the time when the bonds of marriage gave weight to this interpretation. Later he imagined Theseus as entering the Maze assured only by the thread of an inner fidelity. And finally, in the finished work, he shows that Theseus had returned only because he had never broken with his past, because he had clung to the thread of tradition. This is the time when Gide had learnt, through the dangers of war, of the value of the past and of tradition. In his tale he follows, step by step, the path traced by the old legend, drawing his material from Euripides, Plutarch and Racine. Theseus is the last of his heroes—the last also of his bastards, since he was supposed to have been the son not of his reputed father, Aegeus, but of the sea god, Poseidon. Gide tells the well-known story in such a way as to symbolise his own preoccupations and those of humanity. He has even succeeded in rationalising the supernatural events, so that there remains nothing in the tale to strain the belief of even the most materialistic of readers. What is new here, and not in the Greek legend, is Gide's conception of the dangers of the labyrinth; he sees those who venture in as overcome by the fumes, as if of drugs and wine, which make them reluctant to leave it.

New also in Gide's tale is the last meeting between Oedipus and Theseus, when the latter recognises that although he has been successful everywhere, he must acknowledge the former as his equal. Indeed he was at first inclined to think that his own victories were small things in comparison with what Oedipus had accomplished, he who had dared, in the name of man, to throw down a challenge to the Gods. Why then, Theseus asks himself, did he accept defeat? Why indeed, by putting out his eyes, did he contribute to that defeat? That was something Theseus could not understand and, on this meeting, he asked him the question. Oedipus answered that he could turn his anger on no one but himself, and had put out his eyes to punish them for not having seen what they should have seen. But there was something more, Oedipus added; darkness had suddenly become for him another light, and he realised that the world invisible to our senses is the real one; all the rest is only illusion which obscures our contemplation of the divine, and one must cease to see the world in order to see God. Theseus did not deny the importance of the spiritual world, but did not see why it should exclude the material one in which we live and have our being. Oedipus interrupted to say that it is only in suffering that man can accomplish a heroic destiny, that when he falls a victim he forces recognition from Heaven, and disarms the vengeance of the Gods.

Theseus is not convinced and when he is alone he formulates his own *credo*, and we feel that it is Gide himself who is speaking and leaving his own testament to the world. He declares that he remains a child of this old world of ours and that man must play with the cards he holds, that he has nothing else. He says: 'I have built my town. After me my thought will be able to inhabit it eternally. It is consenting that I draw near my solitary death. I have enjoyed the benefits of the earth. It is pleasant for me to think that, after me, and thanks to me, men will find themselves happier, better and freer. For the good of future humanity I have lived.'

For more than five years Gide waited for his own 'solitary death', and, although he wrote nothing new of value, these years were filled in adding further details to his portrait of the grand old man of French literature. He spent his time in preparing his work for publication, writing the final pages of his *Journal*, gleaning the last sheaves from the rich harvest. He spent time also in lectures and travel, preaching a message of hope and courage to the weary and disillusioned post-war young. For Gide, in personal and public matters, defeat is not total tragedy; it is an impulse to continue the struggle for a deeper life. We do not find in his last works the blank despair, albeit noble despair, of a Camus for whom life is an absurd and meaningless farce towards which the only attitude is one of stoic resignation, what he calls sainthood without God.

A young student wrote to Gide after the War telling him that the chief thing he had learnt from his work was that despair is the only dignity left to man. Gide was horrified and much distressed at this travesty of his ideas, and he answered him publicly, saying that absence of faith is pernicious, for there is a meaning in the world, and that it depended on man, that man was responsible for God. He returned to a similar conception in the Bryce Memorial Lecture which he gave in Oxford in June 1947. He took as his text the lines from Vergil where Aeneas is described as fleeing from burning Troy with his aged father on his back. Gide said that these lines should be interpreted symbolically, that Aeneas was not merely bearing his father on his shoulders but the whole weight of his past. In the same way we were fleeing from the burning city of our civilization based on the sanctity of each human soul, and it was our duty to see that it did not perish. Though the city of European culture might be burning we could still preserve its most precious essence.

Unfortunately this lecture exists now only in the memories of those who heard it, for Gide, as soon as it was delivered,

54

destroyed the script because his old friend and adviser, Roger Martin du Gard, had told him it was 'médiocre et insuffisant'.

In June 1947 Gide received his first honour, although he was seventy-eight at the time: the degree of Doctor of Letters, *Honoris Causa*, at the University of Oxford. In November of the same year he was awarded the Nobel Prize for literature.

After *Thésée* there was no further major work, but Gide did not remain idle. He published a prose translation of *Hamlet* which was performed with considerable success in France and abroad; also a stage version of *The Trial* by Kafka which was produced by Jean-Louis Barrault in 1947. In 1949 came a book of essays entitled *Feuillets d'Automne*—a pun on Victor Hugo's *Feuilles d'Automne*—also an anthology of French poetry, with a long introduction on the nature of poetry. During the last two years of his life he took an active part in filming *Isabelle*, and in dramatising *Les Caves du Vatican* which was produced at the Comédie Française; he also appeared in person in a film called *La Vie commence demain*; in January 1950, a year before he died, he read the final passage from *Thésée* on the Radio, which was, as it were, his testament and farewell to life. And finally, also in 1950, he published the last volume of his *Journal*, taking the account up to his eightieth birthday. He did not intend to write any more however long he lived. A born writer however dies hard, and he kept a note-book in which he recorded, without dates or order, the random thoughts that occurred to him. This was published posthumously under the title, *Ainsi soit-il, ou les Jeux sont faits*.

The key-note of the last volume of the *Journal* is serenity, but mingled with sadness; for he knew that he was taking his leave, and that death had slipped in between himself and things, so that the union could no longer be effected. He noticed this without bitterness but only with a certain melancholy.

He was in failing health for the last few years of his life, but did not, even then, lose interest in the problems of the world; for a month before he died, he answered a Japanese scholar, one of the atom-bomb victims of Nagasaki, who had written to ask what attitude man should take on the eve of the conquest of the world by the union of conformism and machines. Gide answered in a long and full letter in which he said that, in spite of everything which had happened, it was to individualism that he clung, it was in individualism that he saw the only hope. The individual, with his hatred of falsehood, offered a solid foundation, a sort of rampart on which to meet and come to an agreement. There lay the only possibility of salvation. 'We are like unto one', said Gide, 'who, to light his way, follows a torch that he himself is carrying'.

At the end of his life Gide reached the complete serenity without which he would have considered it a failure, and he waited with calm for death to come, surrounded by his family of daughter, son-in-law and grand-children whom he loved dearly. In *Feuillets d'Automne*, his last work, he had written:

'Take things as they are, play with the cards one has; insist on being what one is, which does not prevent one from struggling against all the falsehoods, falsifications, that man has imposed on a natural state of affairs against which it is vain to revolt. The acceptance of what can be modified is not contained in the *Amor Fati*, which does not prevent one from expecting from oneself the best, after one has recognised it for such. One does not make oneself more like oneself by giving full expression to the least good.'

Death finally came for him on February 19th, 1951, after a few days of illness. He was buried on February 22nd, in the little country cemetery at Cuverville where his beloved wife lay. He had wished to be buried without religious ceremony, but the protestant rites were read at his grave-side.

Gide did not believe in personal immortality, but even in his own life-time he had become immortal through his works. He had already taken on that shape, as Mallarmé said of Poe, 'tel qu'en lui-même enfin l'éternité ne change'.

Conclusion

Gide was a man who found his own harmony and movement in a duality of polarisation. He needed this perpetual motion to obtain power for creation, just as some writers need to sin to gain the dynamic force of remorse. He had aspirations towards spirituality, asceticism and puritanism; but also leanings towards sensuality, self-indulgence and sin. It was not the contrast and clash between *Spleen* and *Idéal*, which we find in Baudelaire, man's longing for purity and beauty in conflict with his inevitable proclivity towards sin and vice. That was not Gide's problem; his was one of equilibrium and balance. It was necessary for him to find that one point between both poles where he could freely balance, like a see-saw, from one to the other, backwards and forwards, with equal attraction to each, refusing the necessity for blame or remorse when he came down on the side of what is called vice. Yet, at the same time, he desperately needed sanction and approval, and to feel always that he was right. When composing *Corydon* he was not content with merely gaining freedom and immunity for his own instincts, he needed as well the sanction and support of science and history. In the same way, when he had finally accepted atheism, he claimed confirmation for his lack of faith in the Bible itself. This curious twist of his nature was the cause of the accusation of intellectual dishonesty which has so often, unjustly, been made against him. But it came rather from the deep uncertainty in him which no amount of success, no amount of experience, could cure. He needed intellectual sanction to feel that he was right, and to be right was what he wanted more than anything else. But he would not compromise in order to

56

achieve it, and this led him into the contradictory state of desire for martyrdom, which is, in fact, an inverted way of being right. Unable to believe in himself without assurance, he was forced into that vacillation and twisting which are the most characteristic aspect of the Gidian personality. In the same way he had a longing to be loved which no amount of affection could satisfy. When he was young he wrote: 'My constant question—and it becomes an unhealthy obsession—could anyone love me?' And at the end of his life he wrote: 'An extraordinary, an insatiable need to be loved; I believe this is what dominated my life and urged me to write'.

Yet he did not achieve the perfect relationship where love might have blossomed, and in that failure he was not himself without blame. He was always so morbidly afraid that he might be vanquished by woman, by his wife, as he had been in youth by his mother, that he tore himself away, destroying the delicate tendrils which encircled him, before they could bind him. His behaviour to his wife, incomprehensible at times, was an effort to escape intact.

His own affection and sympathy went out to humble, pitiable and unsure beings, to those unfavoured by life. There were the beggar children in Normandy amongst whom he used to sit, reading them the Fables of La Fontaine. They considered him their friend, running to meet him when they saw him in the distance striding along, his full pilgrim's cloak billowing in the wind. He never felt disgust though he had often, when he got home, to shake their vermin from his clothes.

That same sympathy he showed also to unfortunate dumb animals. He used to pick up injured and sick birds in the woods to nurse them back to health in his bedroom, feeding them on drops of milk as if they were delicate babies, and tending them through long nights of crisis; one of these died, and he wrote to a friend: 'He died this morning, the night had been too cold. This little sorrow has made me very gloomy'.

Although Gide was particularly interested in his own problem as an individual, he was passionately interested as well in the larger problem of individualism in the world today. This brought him many of his readers in all parts of the world, those who seek a remedy to our present discontents. The problem of our time, as Gide sees it—the real crisis of our age—is how to reconcile the inalienable right of the individual to self-development, and the urgent necessity for the diminution of the misery of the masses. In these days of collectivity and mass-thinking, when security from the womb to the tomb is the goal, there is the danger that the individual may be strangled in the ever-increasing coils of bureaucratic red tape. For Gide there was no contradiction between belief in the individual and belief in the community—he had hoped to find the reconciliation in Communism—but he would not sacrifice the sanctity of each individual human soul, since he believed that only by being

57

truly himself could man be of service or value to others. He had a horror of the slow ruminating of the herd, pedigree or otherwise, chewing over the same cud of ideas. He preferred to wander and be lost rather than follow the well mapped-out paths. He had the pride of the one lost sheep, safe in the knowledge that the Eternal Shepherd will scour the hillsides to look for him, and that there will be more rejoicing in Heaven at his being brought safely back to the fold, than for the ninety-nine which never strayed.

In his sixty years as a writer there had been a constant evolution in Gide's style of the same order as the transformation which occurred in his thought. At first he was a poet, preoccupied with himself, using language to express personal lyric feelings—there are some who regret the disappearance of this personal artist—and eventually he became a moralist with a style of pure and sober classicism. In his early writings he adopted the musical manner of the Symbolists and favoured 'la chanson grise', which gave full freedom to his imagination. By the end of the First World War, however, he had banished all extraneous ornamentation from his style. One need only compare *La Symphonie Pastorale* with the early works to realise the difference. The complete simplicity of the language now matches the dazzling whiteness of the snow. Later his language became still more stripped and bare as he perfected the art of Racine, of expressing most by saying least, a strict form containing and restraining deep emotion.

Although all through his life Gide went out with eager anticipation towards the future, he remained, after he reached maturity, classical and universal in the truest meaning of the expression, and became a repository of the past, to protect it against destruction. European civilization for him, in spite of Christianity, grew from Graeco-Roman roots; and, although he was interested in foreign literatures, reading and absorbing much from such writers as Dostoevsky, Shakespeare, Blake and Nietzsche, he nevertheless felt deep down that it was in French classical culture that it had reached its most perfect flowering.

After an examination of sixty years and eighty odd volumes of Gide's writings the impression remains that he is a moralist, psychologist and stylist rather than a pure novelist or dramatist. Each of his novels is an attitude which he adopts for the sake of argument, of speculation—he tells us so himself—and that makes him less of a novelist than a moralist; less of a novelist than an investigator. He does not concern himself with creating complex characters giving the illusion of life; he is less interested in *men* than in *man*, in the classical sense. 'Man is more interesting than men', he says, 'it is he whom God has made in his own image'. He is less anxious to make an amalgam of contradictions than to isolate some special characteristic. He is a chemist who isolates certain substances to obtain their purest essence. Each

58

of his works is a chemical experiment in purifying some particular quality or vice which he pursues to its logical conclusion.

La Porte Étroite is probably Gide's most perfect and moving book, but his *Journal* is perhaps his most characteristic and original. It is a work unique in French literature—indeed in any literature; a treasure-house of discussion on every artistic and intellectual movement, on every moral problem, of more than sixty years. As a whole it may lack form and unity—indeed how could it be otherwise, with its million words dealing with so many topics and phases of life; but individual passages are amongst his finest writing. He has written few pages of greater beauty, simplicity and poignancy, than his description of the death of the writer Charles-Louis Philippe, and his funeral amongst the simple peasants who were his family.

Little by little, as we read the *Journal*, a picture of its writer begins to take shape in our minds; not the full-length psychological and critical portrait which, one day, will have to be attempted, but the series of impressions we receive from those whom we frequent with pleasure and sympathy; a picture of a man of rare delicacy, sensitivity and perception; a man more at home with simple and unpretentious people than with the learned or sophisticated; a man of great humility, and singularly lacking in vanity who, until the end of his life, remained shy and unsure of himself and surprised when people thought highly of him. At a lunch given in Oxford in his honour he had to wipe the tears away from his eyes as he replied to the speech of welcome, and he said it was the first honour he had ever received: 'Regardez', he added, 'je n'ai pas de rouge à ma boutonnière'. Of all those who came into close contact with him, although there might be many who, at times, were exasperated and infuriated by him, there were few who did not love him, for he was an eminently lovable man. Only those who knew little of him disliked him.

Gide declared that the whole of his work up to *Les Faux Monnayeurs* was written as a plea to Madeleine; the *Journal* might have been written as a plea to posterity for understanding, not in a cold and detached way, but with sympathy and lack of condemnation. This explains why he did not seek the bitter self-knowledge of a Baudelaire. It was not hypocrisy which led to whatever suppressions there are in the *Journal*. Indeed he feared the accusation of hypocrisy more than any other, and this led him to confess things which others, not necessarily through hypocrisy but often through a sense of human dignity and decency, keep hidden in their hearts. There is no humility in Gide's frankness, but pride, pride that he is able to admit what others do not reveal. That was his special pride.

In spite of all the movements which have come and gone since Gide began to write, in spite of the great changes which world upheavals have wrought, his influence has not ceased to prevail. He relates, in the last volume of the *Journal*, how a young man of twenty-two wrote to him for help, saying that he had struggled for five years against his influence, trying to do what he had advised his readers to do in *Les Nourritures Terrestres*, that is to throw his book away and to leave him behind; but he had to admit: 'I still live with everything you taught me. But I am thirsty. All young people are thirsty with me. You can do something. A glimmer from you might indicate the direction to take—if there is a direction.' Gide answered him that the world would be saved, if indeed it can be saved, only by the unsubmissive. 'Without them it will be all up with our civilization, the culture which we love and which gave a justification to our life on earth. The unsubmissive are the salt of the earth and responsible for God.' Thus the old man of seventy-seven wrote to the youth of twenty-two.

Gide's influence has spread even to the East, witness the letter from the atom-bomb victim of Nagasaki, which has been previously mentioned. All those who sought Gide out hoped that they would find in him help in their distress. There has even been founded a new review by a group of young writers, called *Prétexte*, to express their admiration for him. He would have asked for no better fate than, from beyond the grave, to be able still to speak to the youth of the day.

The tangled skein that is Gide will one day have to be unravelled. There is in everyone, however many the contradictions, one main thread which runs through everything, outlining the individual pattern and making it clear. In Gide it will be found to be a spiritual thread. All through his life, in spite of lapses —even in these lapses—it has been spiritual values that he has always sought, albeit sometimes in the byways. Proust had called his own work, the work of his life-time, *À la Recherche du Temps Perdu*; Gide might have called his *À la Recherche d'une Âme*. 'All our thoughts which have not God for object', he said, 'are of the realm of death'.

Gide's ultimate fate will be to be considered as a moralist in the great French seventeenth-century tradition—the tradition of La Rochefoucauld and Pascal—whose integrity and nobility of thought, whose purity and harmony of style, give him an immortal place amongst the great masters of French literature.

BIOGRAPHICAL NOTES

1869 Gide born in Paris, on the 22nd November, at 19 rue de Médicis.
1880 Death of André Gide's father, at the age of forty-eight.
1889 Gide passes his *Baccalauréat*.
1891 Gide becomes a member of Mallarmé's 'Tuesdays'. Meets Valéry at Montpelier
1893 Gide's first visit to North Africa. He falls ill there and returns to Paris.
1894 Gide's second visit to North Africa.
1895 Death of Gide's mother. He marries his cousin, Madeleine Rondeaux.
1896 Gide elected Mayor of La Roque.
1908 With Jacques Copeau, Jean Schlumberger, André Ruyters and Gaston Galli-
      mard, Gide founds *La Nouvelle Revue Française*.
1914–1915 Gide works at the *Foyer Franco-Belge*, in aid of Belgian refugees.
1918 Gide visits England with Marc.
1922 Gide lectures on Dostoevsky at the Vieux Colombier.
1923 Birth of Catherine, Gide's only child.
1925 Gide's journey to French equatorial Africa.
1936 Gide visits the Soviet Union.
1938 Gide travels to Greece, Egypt and the Senegal. Death of Madeleine Gide.
1939–1942 Gide lives in the south of France.
1942 Gide goes to North Africa.
1944 Gide founds the review *L'Arche*.
1945 Gide returns to Paris.
1945–1946 Gide travels in the Near East.
1947 Gide is given the degree of Doctor of Letters, *Honoris Causa*, by the University
      of Oxford. He is awarded the Nobel Prize for literature.
1950 *Les Caves du Vatican* is produced at the *Comédie Française*.
1951 Gide dies in Paris on the 19th February. He is buried at Cuverville on the 22nd
      February.

BIBLIOGRAPHICAL NOTES

A. List of Gide's works (Those published in English translation are marked
    with an asterisk.)

1891 *Les Cahiers d'André Walter.*
      Le Traité du Narcisse.
      Notes d'un Voyage en Bretagne.
1892 *Les Poésies d'André Walter.*
1893 *Voyage d'Urien.*
      La Tentative Amoureuse.
1895 *Paludes.* The Marshlands.*
1897 *Réflexions sur quelques points de littérature et de morale.*
      Les Nourritures Terrestres.* Fruits of the Earth.
1899 *El Hadj.*
      Le Prométhée mal enchaîné.* Prometheus Misbound.
      Philoctète.
      Feuilles de Route.
1900 *Lettres à Angèle.*
      De l'Influence en Littérature.
1901 *Le Roi Candaule.*
      Les Limites de l'Art.
1902 *L'Immoraliste.* The Immoralist.*
1903 *Saül.*
      Prétextes.
      Oscar Wilde.
      De l'Importance du Public.
1904 *De l'Évolution du Théâtre.*
1906 *Amyntas.* Amyntas.*
1907 *Retour de l'Enfant Prodigue.*
1908 *Dostoevsky d'après sa Correspondance.*
1909 *La Porte Étroite.* Strait is the Gate.*
1911 *Nouveaux Prétextes.*
      Charles-Louis Philippe.
      Isabelle.* Isabella.
1912 *Bethsabé.*
1914 *Souvenirs de la Cour d'Assises.* Recollections of the Assize Court.*
      Les Caves du Vatican.* The Vatican Swindle.
1919 *La Symphonie Pastorale.* Pastoral Symphony.*
1923 *Dostoevsky.* Dostoevsky.*
1924 *Corydon.* Corydon.*
      Incidences.
1926 *Les Faux Monnayeurs.* Coiners.*
      Le Journal des Faux Monnayeurs.* The Logbook of the Coiners.
      Numquid et tu.
      Si le Grain ne meurt.* If it die.
1927 *Voyage au Congo.* Travels in the Congo.*
      Retour du Tchad.* Return from Lake Chad.
1929 *L'École des Femmes.* The School for Wives.*
      Suivant Montaigne.
      Essai sur Montaigne.
      Un Esprit non prévenu.
1930 *Robert.*
      L'Affaire Redureau.
      La Séquestrée de Poitiers.
1931 *Oedipe.* Oedipus.*
1932 *Goethe.*
1934 *Perséphone.*
      Pages de Journal, 1929–1932.
1935 *Les Nouvelles Nourritures Terrestres.* New Fruits of the Earth.*
1936 *Nouvelles Pages de Journal, 1932–1935.*
      Geneviève.
      Retour de l'U.R.S.S.* Back from U.S.S.R.
1937 *Retouches à mon Retour de l'U.R.S.S.* Afterthoughts on the U.S.S.R.*
1938 *Notes sur Chopin.*
1939 *Journal, 1889–1939.* The Journals of André Gide, Vols I–III.*

1941 *Découvrons Henri Michaux.*
1942 *Le Treizième Arbre.*
1943 *Interviews Imaginaires.*
     Attendu que.
1944 *Pages de Journal.** The Journals of André Gide, Vol. IV.
1946 *Thésée.** Theseus.
     Le Retour.
1947 *Paul Valéry.*
     *Le Procès.** The Trial. (a stage version of Kafka's novel.)
1948 *Correspondance, Francis Jammes et André Gide.*
     Préfaces.
     Rencontres.
1949 *Robert ou de l'Intérêt Général.*
     Feuillets d'Automne.
     Anthologie de la Poésie Française.
     *Correspondance, Paul Claudel et André Gide.** Correspondence, Paul Claudel and André
        Gide.
1950 *Journal, 1942–1949.** The Journals of André Gide, Vol. IV.
     Littérature Engagée.
     Lettres de Charles du Bos et Réponses d'André Gide.
1951 *Et nunc manet in te, (Suivi de Journal Intime.)** Et nunc manet in te.
1952 *Ainsi-soit-il ou Les Jeux sont faits.*

B. SELECT LIST OF WORKS DEALING WITH ANDRÉ GIDE.

R. M. Albérès: *L'Odyssée d'André Gide*, 1951.
Paul Archambault: *Humanité d'André Gide*, 1946.
Yvonne Davet: *Autour des Nourritures Terrestres*, 1948.
François Derais et Henri Rambaud: *L'Envers du Journal d'André Gide*, 1951.
Charles du Bos: *Le Dialogue avec André Gide*, 1929.
Ramon Fernandez: *André Gide*, 1931.
Albert Guerard: *André Gide*, 1951.
Jean Hytier: *André Gide*, 1938.
Renée Lang: *André Gide et la Pensée Allemande*, 1949.
Klaus Mann: *André Gide and the Crisis of Modern Thought*, 1948.
Harold Marsh: *André Gide and the Hound of Heaven*, 1952.
Roger Martin du Gard: *Notes sur André Gide*, 1951.
Claude Mauriac: *Conversations avec André Gide*, 1951.
Henri Mondor: *Premiers Temps d'une Amitié*, 1947.
George Painter: *André Gide*, 1951.
Léon Pierre-Quint: *André Gide*, 1932 and 1952.
Paul Souday: *André Gide*, 1927.
D. L. Thomas: *André Gide, the Ethic of the Artist*, 1950.